RUGBY SKILLS, TACTICS & RULES

RUGBY SKILLS, TACTICS & RULES

THIRD EDITION

TONY WILLIAMS & FRANK BUNCE

BLOOMSBURY
LONDON · BERLIN · NEW YORK · SYDNEY

Note:
Whilst every effort has been made to ensure that the content of this book is as technically accurate and as sound as possible, neither the author nor the publishers can accept responsibility for any injury or loss sustained as a result of the use of this material.

First published in the UK in 2008 by
A&C Black, an imprint of
Bloomsbury Publishing Plc
50 Bedford Square
London WC1B 3DP
www.bloomsbury.com

Reprinted in 2010
Third edition 2012

First published in New Zealand in 2008 by
David Bateman Ltd,
30 Tarndale Grove
Albany, Auckland

ISBN 978-1-408-15695-7

Design and typesetting: Trevor Newman Design

Captions:
Pages 2–3: Alesana Tuilagi in full flight.
Pages 4–5: Dominiko Waganiburotu of Fiji and Rocky Elsom of Australia contest the ball.

Printed and bound in China through Colorcraft Ltd, Hong Kong

Acknowledgements: Many thanks to Paul Bateman, editor Caroline List and the editorial and design staff who have worked so hard to produce this book. Thanks to Andrew Cornaga and the Photosport team for the dynamic photos. But thanks most of all to the many enthusiasts around the world who play and support the great game of rugby.

CONTENTS

THE JOY OF RUGBY

You are running with the ball tucked under your arm. Ahead is the open field, uncluttered by opposition, with a white line beckoning; behind you, the thunder of pounding feet. All around are screaming, exhilarated voices. Your legs are thumping. Your heart is pounding. You have never felt so alive. Will they catch you? Or will you score the try . . .

Running with the ball in open space is the ultimate joy in rugby. But there are so many other pleasures: the try-saving tackle; the beautifully timed pass; pushing, pulling and getting muddy; the challenge and adventure of it all; coming off the field soaked in sweat or drenched with rain, knowing that you have given your all and shared not just in the comradeship of your own team, but in that of the opposition as well.

Where else can you have so much fun without getting into trouble? Where else can you have the freedom to run like a racehorse, charging forwards, ball in hand, to pounce in the tackle and reach high in the line out, toil like a coal miner, yet leap as a gazelle to catch the high ball, or smash into the opposition, or weave in and out of them like a bird in flight?

It has been said that rugby is a game for hooligans played by gentlemen (while soccer is a game for gentlemen played by hooligans). It did all start with hooligans, whole villages of them, fighting and competing for an inflated pig's bladder encased in leather, scrums of people, sometimes hundreds of them, pushing and pulling for possession of the prize. Inevitably, rules had to be made to cut down on injuries, even deaths.

In 1823 the rules specified the use of the feet only and it was in defiance of this that William Webb Ellis of Rugby School first picked up the ball and ran with it. Today the ultimate prize in rugby, the Rugby World Cup, is called the Webb Ellis Trophy. So rugby had two births: first, as an unruly game of wild abandon; and the other, as an act of spirited defiance. Both remain at the soul of rugby today, which perhaps explains why there are so many rules and restrictions in today's game, designed to actually permit the use of acceptable and safe levels of force.

Above: *Ma'a Nonu of the world champion All Blacks wears a crown of dreadlocks.*
Left: *Exuberant Canadian fans.*

The Samoans perform their fearsome war dance. Such gladiatorial challenges have become part of the culture of rugby.

Rugby is essentially a gladiatorial contest of strength, speed, deception and skill — some would say only one step removed from actual warfare. The truth is that any player on a rugby field is allowed to do almost anything. The only two things they really are not allowed to do are throw the ball forwards and tackle an opponent dangerously.

Rugby is a game for all shapes and sizes. The legendary Jonah Lomu, once described as "a rhinoceros in ballet shoes" towers over Welsh wizard Shane Williams (who to tackle is like trying to grasp the wind), but Williams has scored more tries than Lomu did in international rugby. And it is also a game for everyone, whatever their country, race, religion or class.

Rugby, also known as Rugby Union or just Union, has itself spawned many offspring. In 1895, Rugby League broke away, altered some of the rules and reduced the number of players allowed on the field from 15 to 13. Rugby Union became Gaelic Football in Ireland, and elsewhere, as Australian Rules football and American Football, it developed into radically different games. There is also a shortened form of the game, Sevens rugby (seven players each side), and there are many forms of touch rugby where tackling is only by a touch.

This book is about Rugby Union, the original game and the most global. It is now played in over 100 countries and the Rugby World Cup is the third biggest sporting event in the world (after the Football World Cup and the Olympic Games), watched by a cumulative worldwide audience of about five billion people.

Anyone new to rugby soon comes to realize that it is more than just a sport. In fact, there are some countries where it is more akin to a religion.

A key factor that sets rugby apart is that it carries its own traditions and values. It harks back to an earlier age when honour and respect were an integral part of combat. In New Zealand, this is manifested in the haka, the fearsome war dance of the international team, the All Blacks (so named because of their black strip). Though to the outsider, the haka might look like an attempt to intimidate, it is actually a Maori tradition that goes back centuries, laying down a challenge to the opposition for them to rise to greater heights. Those who have faced the haka describe it as an eerie experience — they say that the eyes of the All Blacks do not seem to be looking at you, but straight through you.

And to hear Wales sing their national anthem before a match is to go back hundreds of years to the poets of the sixth century who imbued deep and resonant rhythms into the Welsh culture. The anthem France sings before a match, "La Marseillaise", was the rallying call for the French Revolution. It is in ways such as these that, for many, rugby is also a spiritual experience. Other sports also sing national anthems before internationals (the tradition was started at the 1905 match between Wales and the All Blacks), but rugby players almost seem to live them. So it can be said that while all sports exercise the body, rugby also uplifts the spirit.

Above all, rugby is a contest in which every individual can discover more about themselves. International games are not called "test matches" for nothing. Tests are the ultimate challenge; the crucible in which reputations are forged

Rugby is a game for all shapes and sizes. Luke Charteris, Alun Wyn Jones and Shane Williams of Wales singing their national anthem with pride and passion.

and legends are created. Then after the match, when the clashes of battle have stilled, comes the exchanging of stories and laughter and the shared respect and friendship that will last a lifetime.

The purpose of this book is simply to help you become the best player you can be and to get the most enjoyment out of rugby as possible. Some will just play for fun, but some have ambitions to go further and yearn to draw the cloak of honour of an international jersey over their shoulders. It is entirely up to you. Everyone, however, starts at the same place. Before you can run, you have to learn to stand and walk. It is the same with the acquisition of rugby skills. You start with the simplest, learn in steps, and then it is a matter of how fast you learn and how often and hard you practise.

As a child, All Black Dan Carter's parents became so familiar (and probably irritated) with the *thump*, *thump*, *thump* of a rugby ball hitting their roof that they built rugby posts for him at the bottom of the garden and then it was *practise*, *practise*, *practise*.

Note: The terms *law* or *rule* are used interchangeably to describe the laws of rugby. Sometimes law or rule is also used here to mean a general principle, such as the *golden rules of rugby*. It should be clear from the context which is meant.

Above: The enjoyment of schoolboy rugby.

Left: Rugby is a game of contest, collision and getting to know your opponent up close.

Top right: These days rugby fans just love to dress up.

Right: "Man mountain" Brad Thorn (centre) seems to be carrying the world on his shoulders.

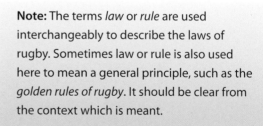

MASTERING THE SKILLS

Rugby Skills, Tactics & Rules starts with the small steps of individual skills first, then moves to unit and team skills and on through to tactics at an easy gradient. And here's a tip — if you have trouble mastering a skill, go back to the last one you thought you had mastered . . . perhaps you didn't quite get it right the first time after all! Now, try again and master it, then move forwards again and you will quickly acquire the skill you had difficulty with previously. (A lot of team moves break down because individual players have not mastered individual skills, such as catching the ball.)

Most sports require a mix of strength, speed and skill. Rugby also requires knowledge, which breaks down into the terrible twins of "terminology" and "technique". Terminology means knowing the meaning of the words, and if you don't know the words, you can't sing the song. There is a lot of terminology in rugby, even if some of it is something as simple as knowing the nicknames that some international teams go by: for example, Springboks (South Africa) and Wallabies (Australia). This book is written in plain English, with a glossary at the back: if you still find your attention wandering, grab a dictionary. The rule is: the better you understand the definition, the better the execution.

In rugby, a key part of your knowledge will be understanding the laws. There are 22 of them and in the official International Rugby Board (IRB) publication they run to 196 pages. At some point, to be the complete rugby player, you will have to get to grips with all of them. But they are written in rather dry, legal English and so to make it easy for you, the content of most of them has been threaded into the text at appropriate places, with clear

Above: *Catch me if you can!*   **Top right:** *Determination etched all over the face of Alisi Tupuailai of Japan.*
Right: *USA vs England Saxons. Rugby is above all a team game.*

To reach the summit, you must touch the earth. Try!

explanations of those old chestnuts that seem to confuse everybody.

At the beginning of the book there is a light-hearted overview of the laws, then at the end, a list of the law numbers with a few oddities pointed out. Understanding the laws better will enable you to play with more confidence and certainty, and give you an advantage over opponents who may only have a vague understanding of them.

Rugby is a highly technical sport, as technical as judo even. Technique is about how the skill is executed. You have to get the technique exactly right to get the desired result. With the correct tackling technique, for example, the smallest player on the field can dump the biggest. Correct technique is also your best guarantee of safety and protection against injury.

You will be most successful if you practise getting each technique as close to perfection as possible. For this, the book suggests many drills. Others you can make up yourself. Do them repetitively without much talk; just action. You should do all drills on a gradient, not moving to the next until you have mastered the previous one. For example, with goal kicking, the gradient would be first kicking close in front of the posts (easy kicks), then further back, at different angles, in difficult wind conditions, then with a teammate approximating the pressure of a match situation, trying to put you off, shouting at you or distracting you by taking potshots at you with a water pistol!

Above all else, this book aims to provide you with the principles and skills to enable you to think for yourself on a rugby field. That is the New Zealand way, which has helped many New Zealand teams, such as the All Blacks, the current world champions, consistently achieve success on rugby playing fields around the world. New Zealand Sevens teams have also won the majority of World Sevens Series titles; the New Zealand women's team, the Black Ferns, have won four consecutive World Cups; New Zealand players are regularly selected for other international teams (after they have served three years' residency), and New Zealanders often coach other international teams, such as three of the four semi-finalists in the 2011 Rugby World Cup (New Zealand, Australia and Wales).

Above: *Happiness is being covered in mud.*

Left: *Surrounded by teammates, All Black captain Richie McCaw holds aloft the ultimate rugby trophy, the Webb Ellis Rugby World Cup, October 2011.*

Below, left: *Rugby is a family game — Springbok John Smit and children.*

Below: *Small fan, big smile, bigger hair.*

THE GOLDEN RULES OF RUGBY

1. Rugby is played with the ball in hand.
2. Rugby is played on the feet.
3. The ball is faster than the man.
4. Never let a rugby ball bounce.
5. Rugby is a game of contest and continuity.
6. Rugby is a game of possession and territory.
7. The keys are position, possession and pressure.
8. Execute every action at speed.
9. You can defend against everything except pace.
10. Train harder than you have to play.
11. Who wins the contact wins the game.
12. Support play wins matches.
13. Forwards win the game, backs decide by how much.
14. The team that wins is better prepared and hungrier.

THE ALL BLACKS

By percentage of matches won, the All Blacks are the most successful team in any sport anywhere in the world — the winning percentage usually hovers around 80 per cent. The hallmarks of the All Black game are simplicity, technique, unity, pride and a hunger to win.

Rugby took root in New Zealand in 1870 when it was still a pioneer country of tight-knit, hardy communities that fostered many of the qualities of teamwork, Maori warrior spirit, robustness and a practical, down-to-earth attitude which still persist today — qualities which have been augmented by the vigourous cultures of the many Pacific Island people who have settled in New Zealand in more recent times. In general, New Zealanders value fairness and equality, an attitude reflected in its rugby teams where there are no stars — the unity of the team is all. When the All Blacks are running with the ball, it is often noticeable how many players are running in close support, as if they are joined by an invisible thread.

Technique is nigh-on worshipped; there is no greater insult than to say a player's body position is too high. Contact, too, is always robust. One year, when the All Blacks played Scotland, the Murrayfield stand was being rebuilt so that the journalists had to sit near the touchline. Afterwards one of them wrote that he had never realized before how hard the All Blacks hit the contact area. The best All Black sides are also very mobile, they play at pace, attacking in relentless waves, constantly shifting the point of attack and ruthless in execution.

The All Blacks are known to have a certain ethos, an unwritten culture and way of thinking all of their own, which is engraved on the heart of every All Black, and every child who dreams of becoming one. Embodied in this is the imperative to do the black jersey proud and to do your duty by your teammates.

The New Zealand public also expects each new generation to at least match the standards set by their predecessors — and, of course, to win every game! Even that, however, is not good enough. They must perform to the All Blacks' standards; a benchmark that other rugby-playing nations aspire to. That level is a crisp and ruthless execution — as close to perfection as you can get.

1 RUGBY IS A TEAM SPORT

GETTING STARTED

A scratch game of rugby

For an impromptu game of rugby with friends, all you need is a ball, an open patch of ground and four objects to mark out a rectangle. The narrow ends of it are the try lines (where you score) and at the sides are the touchlines (where the ball is out).

The rules are simple:

- the ball is not to be thrown forwards;
- you can tackle an opponent by grasping them and stopping them or bringing them to the ground (but you can't tackle above the shoulders);
- if play comes to a halt inside the playing area, then it is restarted by an equal number of players from each team having a pushing contest to get possession of the ball (scrum);
- the team that did not cause the halt gets to put the ball in;
- if the ball is sent off the playing area by one team, then play is restarted by the other team throwing the ball back in and an equal number of players from each team have a jumping contest to get possession of the ball (line out).

The above, and having fun, are the essence of rugby.

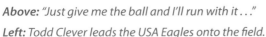

Above: "Just give me the ball and I'll run with it . . ."
Left: Todd Clever leads the USA Eagles onto the field.

. . . but you can't knock or throw the ball forward.

The ground — the four zones

If you want to play a real game, you need a real ground. On the next page there is a diagram of a rugby field. It is basically a big rectangle with a set of tall posts at each end. What a lot of people don't realize is that a rugby field consists of four distinct zones. They are:

1. The field of play: the main area where most of the action takes place.
2. In touch: everything off the field of play. This is defined for one very important reason — the outside lines of a rugby field are OFF the field of play.
3. The 22: the defensive zones 22 metres (about 25 yards) out from each goal line, which have some special defensive rules.
4. In-goal: the zones at each end of the field where the tries (the rugby equivalent of American Football's touchdowns) are scored.

The lines

Don't worry too much about the broken lines at this stage; when they come up during the course of the book you can refer back to this diagram. The following are the main lines to identify now:

• The halfway line cuts the field in half.
• The 22-metre line effectively cuts the field into quarters.
• The goal lines are what the goalposts stand on.
• The touchlines are the outside lines of the field of play. Touch them and the ball is out.
• The touch-in-goal lines are where the touchlines continue into the in-goal. Touch and out!
• The dead-ball lines are the lines at each end. Touch them and the ball is dead (out).

Out! Do you get the important point? Touch any part of the outside lines with the ball or when holding the ball and it is out!

Score a try on the try line: following the same principle, the other outside line of the field of play is the goal line (try line) which puts it in the in-goal.

Drills

1. Trace your finger over each of these lines to familiarize yourself with them.
2. Run along each of the main lines of a rugby field.
3. Run inside the touchline without touching it.
4. Score tries on the goal line.
5. Score tries in the in-goal close to but not touching the touch-in-goal lines and dead-ball line.

The Objective

The laws state: "The object of the game is that two teams, each of 15 players, observing fair play, according to the Laws and in a sporting spirit should, by carrying, passing, kicking and grounding the ball, score as many points as possible."

The Field Markings & Zones

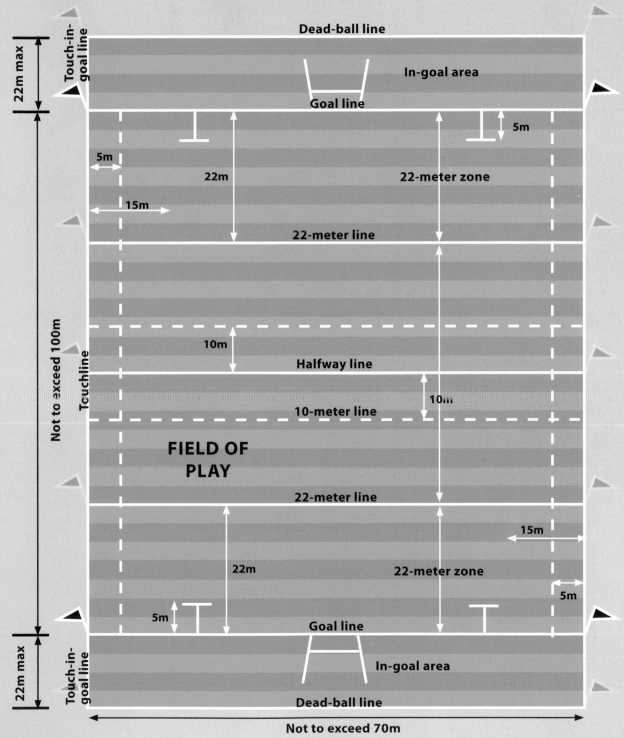

Dead-ball line

In-goal area

Goal line

22m max

Touch-in-goal line

5m

22m

22-meter zone

15m

22-meter line

Not to exceed 100m

Touchline

10m

Halfway line

10m

10-meter line

FIELD OF PLAY

22-meter line

15m

22m

22-meter zone

5m

5m

Goal line

22m max

Touch-in-goal line

In-goal area

Dead-ball line

Not to exceed 70m

A LIGHT-HEARTED OVERVIEW OF THE LAWS OF RUGBY

Once upon a time there was an inflated pig's bladder, encased in leather, and it was thought to be so valuable that lots of men fought for possession of it, so rules were created so they could agree on what they were actually doing and how they would go about it. So touch the goal line (try line) with the ball and it is a try!

Now all that was left to argue about was the interpretation of the rules. Over and above the rules, however, is the spirit of the game. The spirit of rugby tends to be wild and defiant yet still respectful of others.

A game lasts 80 minutes (two halves of 40 minutes each) and the point is to get the ball, by muscle, speed or guile, into the opponent's den (in-goal) and score a try, worth 5 points. This gives you a "try" at kicking a goal (which is the original meaning of the word try). If you are successful "converting" the try by getting the ball over the crossbar of the goal (a conversion), you get another 2 points. With 3 points for a drop goal (field goal) or a penalty kick over the crossbar, the team that has the most points at the end wins the match.

Any player can do anything they like on a rugby field and play as hard as they like within the rules. The only exception is that for safety reasons only front-row players can play in the front row of the scrum (no one else would want to anyway — it's dark in there).

Play is meant to be continuous, but in reality there are stoppages. There is a "constructive" stoppage when one team scores, which is followed by a restart. Then there are the stoppages that come about because a player has violated a law.

The key laws are:
- you are not allowed to knock (knock-on) or throw the ball forwards (forward pass) with your hands or arms;
- you are not allowed to tackle in a dangerous way; and
- you are not allowed to be where you are not supposed to be (offside).

The purpose is to score a try.

You must be kidding! The ref's decision is final.

When players break the rules by accident on the field (such as a forward pass), play is restarted with a throw into a scrum (pushing contest). When players break the rules by causing the ball to go off the field, play is restarted with a throw into a line out (jumping contest). The team that did not break the law gets to throw in.

When a player breaks the rules more forcefully (foul play), a penalty is awarded against their team and the referee might even send the player to the sin bin for 10 minutes (yellow card) or send them off for the rest of the game (red card).

However, if the team that is offended against has an advantage, the referee will allow play to continue because the senior law in rugby is "advantage" to achieve the senior purpose which is keeping the game continuous.

There are pauses (not stoppages) in the game when tackles are made and both teams compete for the ball. In all areas of the game, the contest for possession of the ball is one of rugby's key features. Competing players can try and push each other off a ball lying on the ground. This is a ruck.

If three or more players compete wrestling or pushing for the ball in hand, this is a maul.

The players do all this with full vigour and sportsmanship. The referee makes sure they play to the laws of the game. Which brings us to the last word in the laws: the referee's decision is final, so there!

Drill

Play "Anything-goes" rugby with friends. There are no rules except you are not allowed to hit, kick or choke. You can use a ball or an old towel or a rag — any suitable object will do. You all wrestle for possession of it, everybody against everybody else, no limit on numbers, the only goal being possession, until you are too exhausted or laughing too much to continue.

Above & below: Win the contest for the ball . . . then run with it! French captain Thierry Dusautoir does just that in the France vs Wales 2011 Rugby World Cup semi-final.

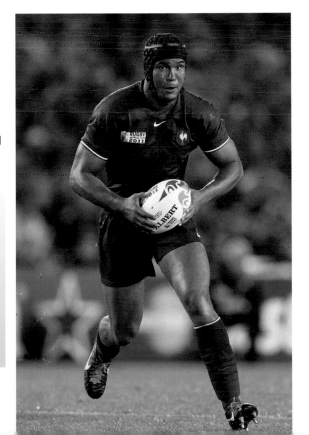

THE TEAM

Rugby is a team game. Tries are scored by individuals, but they are "created" by teams. The definition of a team is: a group with differing roles working together towardss a common purpose. A rugby team consists of 15 players on the field with up to seven replacements off it.

Forwards & backs

The 15 players of a rugby team are divided into forwards (8 players) and backs (7 players). Forwards are usually heavier and go forwards to win the ball; backs are usually faster and stay back to run with it. Refer to the diagram on page 25.

Rugby is a game of confrontation. Here Tonga's Aleki Lutui confronts the French number eight in their 2011 Rugby World Cup pool match.

Forward units

Forwards and backs are subdivided into units. The units in the forwards are defined by the three rows they form in the scrum: front row (3 players), the second row (2), and the back row (3).

Back units

The backs can also be divided into three units, based on how far they stand from the scrum: the halves (2) stand in close to direct their team's play, the centres (2) who defend the middle of the field; and the "back three" (3); the two wings and the fullback who stand at the edges and deep. They are called the "back three" because they often stand back to catch opposition kicks.

Units within units

These then might form other units, depending on what is required. For example, in the scrum the first two rows are often known as the "tight five" because they do more of the tight contact work, while the back row of the scrum who range wider are known as the "loose forwards" or "loosies".

Another way of dividing up the team is into three units: the tight five, the middle five (last three forwards and the first two backs), and the back five (the last five backs). The groupings chosen depend on the strategy being used. Also, as situations develop in a match, there is constant interaction and players will form many different types of units. A centre and wing, for example, form an attacking unit, with the centre seeking to put the wing away to score tries.

Drill
Watch a match and note how many different units are formed during a game.

The Team Positions

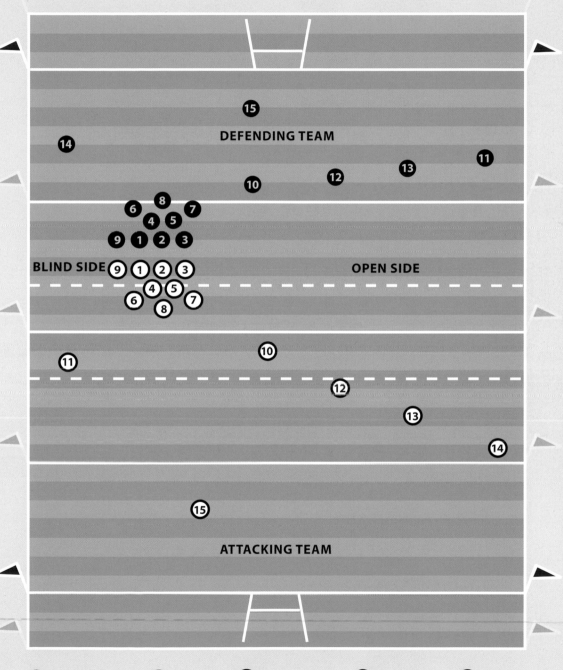

DEFENDING TEAM

BLIND SIDE   OPEN SIDE

ATTACKING TEAM

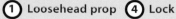

① Loosehead prop	④ Lock	⑦ Open-side flanker	⑩ Fly half	⑬ Outside centre
② Hooker	⑤ Lock	⑧ Number eight	⑪ Wing	⑭ Wing
③ Tighthead prop	⑥ Blind-side flanker	⑨ Scrum half	⑫ Inside centre	⑮ Fullback

Rugby is a game of running — South African Sevens player Mpho Mbiyozo pursued by Canada.

The basic skills

Every player has the same basic skills: running, tackling, passing, catching and attitude. In addition, each player has specialized skills for their positions, their units and whether they are forwards or backs. Then the units have skills as a group. The forwards and backs have skills as their own groups. Finally, the team has skills as a whole team (such as chasing a kickoff).

The positions

The position in a rugby team tells a player where they stand on the field, how to fit into a team and what their duties are. The names for the positions often vary between the northern and southern hemispheres. Down south, the backs are measured in fractions by how far they stand from a scrum; from halfback through five-eighths to fullback. This book uses the most common term worldwide for each position. Just translate them to the term you are familiar with. Starting from the front row of the scrum, here are the positions, their alternative names and jersey numbers. On a rugby field, players are numbered from left to right. Also refer to the diagram on page 25.

POSITIONS WITH ALTERNATIVE NAMES

1, 3	Prop
2	Hooker
4, 5	Second row or lock
6, 7	Flanker, wing forward or loosie
8	Number eight or loosie
9	Scrum half or halfback or half
10	Fly half, first five-eighth or pivot
12	Inside centre or second five-eighth
13	Centre
11, 14	Wing, winger or wing three-quarter
15	Fullback

A scrum is a pushing contest. This one has been won by the All Black forwards.

HOW TO PICK AN AGE-GROUP TEAM BASED ON BASIC SKILLS

Prop — two most solidly built (not fast runners or they'd be backs)

Hooker — solidly built and a good line-out thrower

Locks or **Second row** — the two tallest

Flankers — fittest of the forwards

Number eight — forward who is big, fit and skilful

Scrum half — best long passer

Fly half — best kicker and tactician

Centres — best tacklers and passers

Wings — the two fastest runners

Fullback — best catcher of the high ball

A front row consists of three strong players.

Props

The word prop means "to hold up or support". In France a prop is a *pilier* — a pillar. Props support the hooker in a scrum or a jumper at the line out and at kick restarts. A prop needs strength and good technique.

Loosehead prop

The prop on the left of the scrum (1) is called the loosehead prop because when the scrums engage, this prop has the "loose" (free) head on the outside of the scrum. This is the side where the scrum half puts the ball in and the loosehead's job is to keep the scrum up to make sure his hooker gets a good view of the ball.

Tighthead prop

The prop on the right side of the scrum (3) is called the tighthead prop because their head is "tight" in the scrum between the heads of the opposing hooker and prop. The tighthead's job is to keep the scrum firm and steady on their team's put-in, but to try to disrupt the opposition scrum when it is their put-in.

Winning a tighthead

Because the ball is put into the scrum on the loosehead side, if the other team wins it, that is called a tighthead.

The ideal front row

Because of the dynamics (energies and pressures) of the scrum, ideally the tighthead prop would be the tallest in the front row, followed by the hooker, and the loosehead prop would be the shortest.

> **Drills**
> * Shoulder against shoulder, have a one-on-one pushing contest with a friend.
> * Strength training when younger — swimming and physical work which does not stiffen the muscles.
> * Strength training when older (teens and beyond) — weight training.

Hooker

A hooker is a prop with specialized tasks; to "hook" the ball back in the scrums with their foot and to throw the ball in at the line out. Many hookers also have cheeky personalities. Maybe it comes from being trapped in the middle of a group of 15 other players!

> **Drills**
> * Same as for props.
> * Throwing — aim at a target, throwing a rugby ball over the shoulder.

Second row

The second row is often called the "engine room" or the "boiler house" of the team because they are the ones who give most of the forward thrust at the scrums. That means they have to be strong. They are also the main jumpers at the line out, so they have to be tall. The best second rows are like walking trees.

Drills
- *As for props.*
- *Jumping to touch the crossbar of the goalposts.*

Flankers

The flankers are on each side of the scrum. When the ball comes out, they are the first to pursue it, so they have to be fit and strong. As in the diagram on page 25, there is usually a bigger gap on one side of the field than the other. The wider gap is the "open side". The smaller gap is the "blind side". Though teams sometimes play "right" and "left" flankers, most teams play with open- and blind-side flankers.

Open-side flanker

The open side flanker binds on whichever side of the scrum has the widest gap to the touchline, whether that is left or right. Fitness, support play, tackling and mental alertness are the keys skills of the open-side flanker; also getting to their feet after making a tackle (so they can compete for the ball).

Blind-side flanker

Same as the open-side, except always packs down on the blind side. Usually bigger and not as fast as the open-side. If tall, is often a third jumper in the line out. Ideally a cross between a second row forward and an open-side flanker.

Number eight

At the back of the scrum, the number eight links the forwards to the backs. Usually the strongest player in the back row, the best number eights develop an almost telepathic understanding with the nearest back, the scrum half. The number eight often picks the ball up from the back of the scrum and runs with it, so must be strong at taking the ball forwards.

Back-row drills
- *Running for fitness.*
- *Tackling practice (see tackling section, page 64–65).*
- *Falling to the ground and "bouncing" back to their feet again.*

A second row needs two tall players.

Halfbacks —the "mind" of the team

It is the job of the scrum half and the fly half to control the game to the advantage of their team.

Scrum half

Often the smallest player on the team, as they have to bend low to pick up the ball off the ground and pass it. A quick, long, accurate pass off each hand is their main skill. They should also be quick thinkers, confident and communicative, to link with the other backs and to tell the forwards how to deliver the ball. Scrum halves should run with the ball themselves at least once a half to keep the opposition defence "honest" and whenever an opportunity arises.

Drills
- *Long passing to teammates running onto the ball.*
- *Sprint training over very short distances to develop explosive acceleration.*

Fly half

The fly half is also known as the pivot because everything revolves around them for their team. They are the key creative player and must be able to read the game so that when they receive the ball from the scrum half, they know whether they are going to run, pass or kick it. They should be able to kick with either foot, accurately and long distances. They are often lighter on their feet and so can break through the defensive line with little side steps, jinks and darts. Every great team needs a great fly half.

Drills
- *Study games until you can learn to read the game and so can often predict what will happen next.*
- *Practise catching the scrum-half pass.*
- *Kicking (see kicking section page 78).*

The forwards win the ball and the scrum half back gets it out to the backs.

The backs run with it. Shane Williams of Wales pursued by Manu Tuilagi of England.

Centre

As with the flankers, teams can play a left and right centre, but most play an inside centre and an outside centre (inside meaning closer to the scrum or line out). In back play, the contact area is usually in the centres, so they have to be strong ball carriers and good tacklers. It is often good to have a mix of one strong "battering ram" centre and the other more skilled at creating doubt in the minds of the opposition. Both should be good passers of the ball, especially the outside centre, whose main job is to time the pass to give their wing time and space to score.

Drills
- *Running the ball into tackle bags.*
- *Tackling.*

Wing

The wings should be the fastest runners on the team. Their main jobs are to score tries, chase kicks and catch and return opposition kicks.

Fullback

A fullback tackles like a centre, runs like a wing, and reads the game and kicks like a fly half. They should be good at catching a high ball, especially under pressure. They should be skilled at coming into the back line to create an "extra player" on attack.

Drills — fullback and wing
- *Sprint training.*
- *Catching the high kick (and in wind and rain).*

2 BASIC SKILLS — RUNNING

There are five basic rugby skills that every player should possess: running, passing, catching, tackling and attitude. Together these are the foundations of the game and define the spirit of the team.

RUNNING SKILLS

Running is the most basic skill of all — and it is a skill. Before a player can do anything they have to be fit enough to get to the ball. That requires a player to be responsible for their own fitness and run in their own spare time. There are also skills involved in how to run during a game:

Run straight & hard

The All Black way is to run straight and hard. With amateur players, the tendency is to drift across the field. This effectively makes the field narrower for the attacking team; which is exactly what the defending team wants. Straight running forces the opposition back, draws in the defenders and leaves space on the outside in which to make an attack. Evade enough to avoid the immediate tackler but, in general, run straight.

Run towards support

When running ahead or breaking through the opposing defence, ball carriers should always be aware of the position of their support players and take the line that allows their support players to link up with them.

Support play

Support play wins matches whether it is taking the last pass to score in attack or covering across to make the try-saving tackle in defence. In tight play, support players track closer to the ball carrier but always a few paces behind to enable the ball carrier to offload if halted. This is where fitness really counts. An attack only really runs out of steam when it runs out of support players.

Above: *Close support play wins matches.*

Left: *Run straight and hard.*

Run clever

A player should come off the field with the satisfaction that they have given their all, but should also develop instinct and prediction about the play, so that they don't always run to where the ball is or was, but where it will be.

CARRYING THE BALL

The ball can be carried in one hand or two. The advantage of two is that it gives the ball carrier options to pass or kick and it also casts doubt in the minds of the opposition. A player can run faster with the ball in one hand (pulled tight into their chest unless they have large hands), so that is best for sprinting. If a tackler approaches the side the ball is on, the ball carrier should transfer it to the other hand.

Drills
- *Carrying the ball in one and two hands, practise interchanging and transferring.*
- *Carrying the ball into contact (suitably padded) and protecting the ball.*

The fend-off or hand-off

With the free arm, the ball carrier pushes the tackler away (but not on the head or neck).

The forward charge

With the ball held in one hand the player, leading with the other shoulder, charges forwards straight at an opponent, seeking to blast through them or, at least, commit them to the tackle.

The hit & spin

A version of the forward charge where there is partial contact (intentional or accidental) enabling the ball carrier to "spin" out of the tackle and continue forwards.

The bump

Another version of the forward charge, but in this case the ball carrier slows before impact and lowers their shoulder (and therefore their centre of gravity) to bump the tackler backwards. Then the ball carrier continues. Usually only done successfully by a big player.

Left: Running with the ball in two hands keeps opponents guessing.

Top right: All Black Tony Woodcock has moved the ball to one hand to fend off the tackler.

Right: All Black Joe Rokocoko lowers his shoulder to try and bump off the tackle of Wallaby Berrick Barnes.

DECEPTIVE RUNNING

Pace is effective in open space, but often that space has to be created first. This is usually done by deception. If you can surprise a tackler and make them think, their body also stops which often causes them to shift their balance onto one foot (not evenly balanced between two). There are several ways to run deceptively.

Change of pace

Slow down and the tackler has to as well; then speed up and you will find they will be a fraction behind you.

The drift

A variation on a change of pace in which the ball carrier starts to drift slightly to the side, trying to draw the tackler off balance.

The full stop

Come to a complete stop, momentarily, then speed up again.

Above: Emosi Vucago of Fiji is well balanced to beat an opponent.

Above: Lighter on his feet, All Black Zac Guildford has flat-footed the heavier Springbok forward.

Left: What is Wallaby James O' Connor going to do? Even his teammate Adam Ashley-Cooper doesn't know!

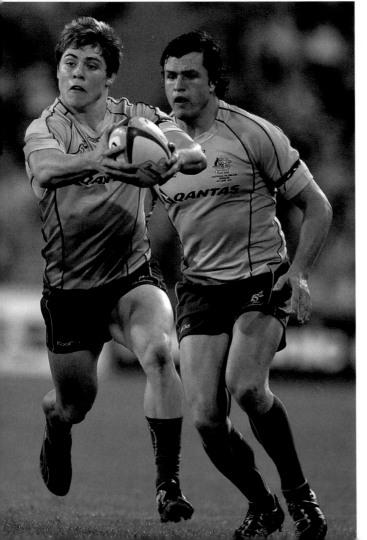

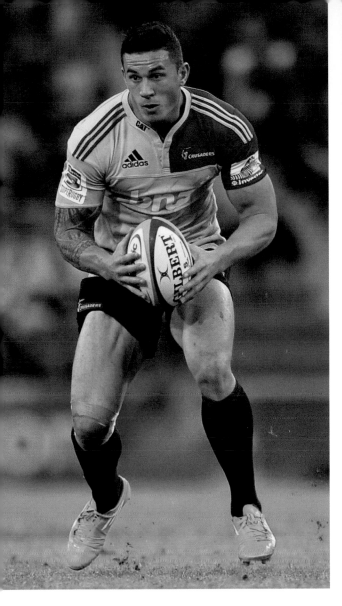

Left: Sonny Bill Williams sets to step.

Above: Ma'a Nonu plants his left foot and drops his left shoulder to step right.

Below: Wallaby Kurtley Beale's direction causes Tomas O' Leary of Ireland to plant his right foot. Beale then sidesteps the other way.

The goose step

Used by the great Australian wing David Campese; slow down, then take two or three quick steps with the knees locked to confuse the tackler, then take off again.

The swerve

The attacker runs straight at the tackler but about three or so paces away starts to curve away, still running fast, and passes beyond the tackler's reach.

Dodge or dart or cut

A very sudden change of direction to the left or right, away from the tackler.

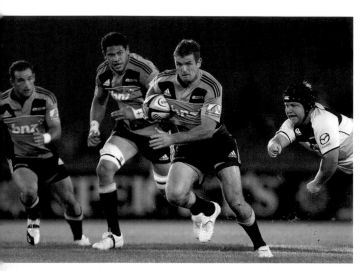

Above: Gliding out of reach of the tackler.

Poetry in motion — ball in two hands, poise, balance, vision.

Outside cut or in-and-out

A mix of change of pace, cut and swerve. The ball carrier slows, cuts back towards the defender then, as they hesitate or set to tackle, the ball carrier runs outside again and sprints away.

The feint

Dropping the shoulder to suggest the ball carrier is going to run one way, but they then go in a different direction.

The side step or step

The side step causes the tackler to plant their balance on one foot. Before contact, the ball carrier takes two or three short stuttering light-footed steps and drops a shoulder to imply they are going one way. As soon as the tackler takes the bait, the ball carrier goes the other way.

The prop

A version of the side step which is heavier footed, with a harder push off the ground with the step, causing the ball carrier to go wider around the tackler.

Change of angle

Teams usually face each other. By receiving the ball or joining an attack at an angle, the attacker can take the defenders by surprise.

Drills
- A game of tag, tiggy or other childhood games using evasion.
- Slalom — create an obstacle course, then run through it, weaving in and out of the obstacles evasively.
- Practise all of the above skills alone, then with friends or teammates.

Perfect balance executed at pace; tackler clutches grass and looks to the heavens.

3 BASIC SKILLS — PASSING

Passing is the major attacking skill in rugby. It is what links the players.

THE THEORY OF PASSING

In rugby, the ball cannot be passed forwards. It can only be passed in a line level with the receiver or behind that line. Always aim to pass backwards, because to pass it level is to risk the referee calling it forward. Most passes use the whole body, some are just a flick of the wrists, some are improvised. Any pass that moves an attack forwards is a good pass. Tries are scored when passing is crisp and accurate.

Creating the extra man

By passing the ball, the attackers try to create a space on the field where they have more players than the defenders do — an overlap — and so are able to go on to score.

When to pass

Pass to a teammate who is in a better position. That means one who is less likely to get tackled and has more opportunity to move forwards with the ball. See the diagram below.

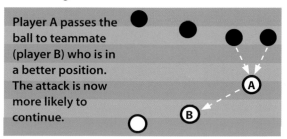

Player A passes the ball to teammate (player B) who is in a better position. The attack is now more likely to continue.

Holding onto the ball

The general rule is, if there is no teammate in a good position to pass to, you hold onto the ball. In other words, the ball carrier is actually in the better position.

Bad pass & hospital pass

A bad pass is one where the receiver is in a worse position and more likely to get tackled. A hospital pass is a very bad pass where the receiver gets completely floored by the tackler as soon as they get the ball and could end up where the name suggests.

Above: If no pass is available, hold onto the ball.
Left: Dan Carter sets to pass.

Present the pass

Some younger players think pass means "sling the ball away when a tackler comes near". But a pass should be like a birthday present, gift-wrapped and dropped right into the receiver's hands.

Aim the pass

You have to either look or know where the receiver is. Aim to get the ball in front of their chest. If they are running onto the ball, this will be forward of their current position.

Passing technique

Usually the whole body swings in one fluid motion. The player holds the ball in two hands, then, like a pendulum, the arms first swing the opposite way before swinging back across the body again in the direction of the pass. Standing still, the feet are placed about the width of the hips. There is a slight sway of the hips. Running, the body falls away from the direction of the pass. There should be minimal break in stride, as the passer now has to run in support of the receiver. At point of release, the passer's hands will be aimed at the target of the pass.

Timing the pass

Timing is everything. By speeding up or delaying the pass the ball carrier might be able to create more time and space for the receiver, especially close to the opposition goal line where such fine adjustments might disrupt the patterns of the defence and result in a try.

Drawing the player

A key skill in timing the pass is to draw the defender, which means running straight at the defender to commit them to the tackle, and then releasing the ball to a teammate just before contact.

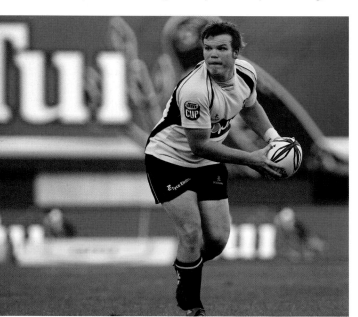

1. The eyes aim at the target, the ball is drawn back the opposite way.

2. The foot is planted and the arms swing in the direction of the pass.

Drills

- *Ball familiarization — look at and inspect the ball thoroughly, so that you are completely familiar with its weight, shape and feel.*
- *Ball handling — toss the ball into the air and catch it, flick the ball around in various ways until you feel happy with it.*
- *Throw the ball over your head and turn and catch it.*
- *Toss the ball back and forth with a teammate, getting progressively further apart.*
- *Walk in a line with teammates passing to the left and right.*
- *Jog in a line with teammates passing to the left and right.*
- *Run in a line with teammates passing to the left and right.*
- *Use two attackers against one defender to draw and pass.*

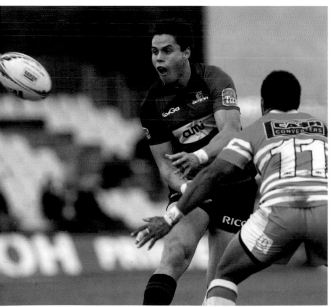

3. The ball is released before the tackler can make contact.

4. (top) Use the whole body to send the pass.
5. (above) When the ball is released, the hands should be aiming at the target.

Passing on

Passing on means to shift the ball out wide quickly even when there are no tacklers in front of the passer, because an advantage might exist out wide.

Passing in wet or very cold weather

In wet weather, passes should be shorter and more care should be taken with accuracy.

TYPES OF PASSES

Long pass

Any pass that is thrown a long distance.

Spin or spiral pass

As the pass is thrown, one hand comes over the top of the ball, causing it to spin through the air. This reduces air resistance and so the pass can be thrown further and quicker.

Scrum-half pass

A specialized, long pass used to send the ball to the backs after a set play. It must be done in one fluid action before the opposition defensive line can come up. Any delay, such as the scrum half taking a step, loses valuable fractions of a second. So before the ball is even in their hands, the scrum half sets themself "cocked ready, like a gun". If the ball is on the ground at a scrum, to pass left, the scrum half's right foot is placed to the right of the ball. The other foot is positioned about a hip's width away, pointing towards the receiver. The knees are slightly bent. The arms are extended so that as soon as the scrum half touches the ball, they can immediately hurl it in one sweeping motion. Spin is usually added for speed and distance by bringing the rear hand over the ball. If the scrum half passes to the other side, these positions are reversed. If the scrum half is upright and receives the ball directly into their hands (such as at a line out) the actions are similar but more upright.

Morgan Parra the French scrum half passes from the base of the scrum.

Reverse pass

A variation of the scrum-half pass when the scrum half finds themselves in a position with their back to the receiver. The ball starts high, held with both hands in front of the chest, before being swung in the direction of the receiver. The hand furthest from the receiver releases the ball early; then the other hand sweeps it in the intended direction, coming over the top of it to give it spin as it is released. Of course, the passer has to be aware of where the receiver is standing. This pass is actually easier to learn than it might seem and when executed properly looks spectacular.

Dive pass

A quick pass used when the scrum half has not been able to get into the proper position for a long pass as above and is under pressure from defenders. The scrum half dives forwards and throws the ball at the same time. The ball is gripped in both hands and thrown from below the waist, through the length of the upper body in a scooping motion and released when the passer's arms are fully stretched. After the pass, the scrum half will naturally end up on the ground. The scrum-half pass and dive passes are not restricted to use by scrum halves. They can be done by anybody as the situation demands.

Fast pass

The ball is fired out at extra speed.

Lob pass

A high, looping toss of the ball over the heads of defenders to a teammate.

Pop pass

A short, looped pass that sits in the air for a teammate coming through at pace.

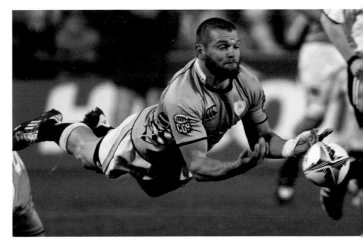

Above: Dive pass. Ball scooped from below the waist and hands end up in front of the chest.

Below: All Black Piri Weepu flicks the ball out the back.

Flick pass

A short pass thrown quickly with a flick of the wrists.

The offload

Passing the ball in the tackle by any means possible. All Black Sonny Bill Williams is the "king" when it comes to this sort of improvised passing.

Above: An overhead pass by Nick Easter of England.

Below: Tackled and going to ground, but Ireland's Paul O' Connell still gets his pass away.

One-handed pass

Passing the ball using one hand, usually because the other is tied up in the tackle.

Overhead pass

The ball is held high in one hand and thrown over a defender's head to a teammate.

The reverse flick

A player running forwards knows — or gets a call — that a teammate is following behind. Without looking, the passer flicks the ball back to them out of the back of their hand. A very instinctive pass which can be devastating when effective because it is so unexpected.

The "anything goes" pass

Getting the ball to your teammate any which way you can.

DECEPTIVE PASSES

There are a number of ways of deceiving the opposition by NOT passing the ball.

The dummy pass or dummy

Also known as "throwing" or "selling a dummy". The ball carrier goes through all the motions of passing the ball, but holds onto it and keeps running. The trick is in the selling. If the attacker believes themselves that they are going to pass, then usually so will the defender.

The non-pass

A version of the dummy. The ball carrier, running at speed, slows slightly as if about to pass, then when the defender hesitates, suddenly takes off again.

The dummy kick

Similar to the dummy, the ball carrier pretends to be about to kick. When the tackler hesitates, the attacker holds onto the ball and keeps running.

Change-of-direction pass

The ball carrier is about to pass the ball one way but instead holds on to it, twists around and passes it in another direction.

Decoys or decoy runners

Decoys are players who run as though they are going to take a pass. Decoys are useful for confusing the opposition's defence.

As defenders converge, All Black Mils Muliaina passes the ball to keep it alive.

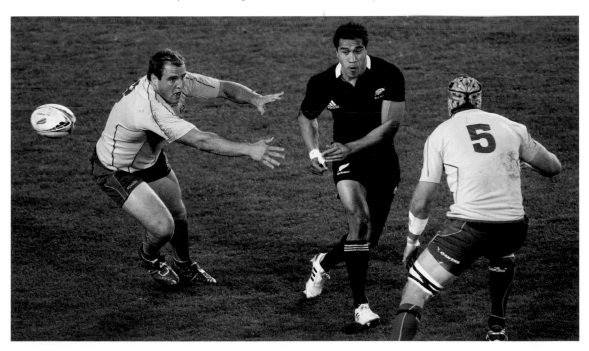

4 BASIC SKILLS — CATCHING

Catching is all about accepting the ball and bringing it under control.

GOLDEN RULE OF CATCHING

The key or motto to catching is to keep your eye on the ball. Always watch the ball until it is safely into your hands. Concentrate on this before doing anything else, including thinking about what you are going do with it next.

To catch or not to catch

First you have to make the decision to catch the ball. If it is out of comfortable reach, you have to decide whether or not you can take it. It might be better to leave it than risk a knock-on.

Knock-on

A knock-on is when the ball hits a player anywhere between the hand and the arm and then strikes the ground or an opposing player. The referee awards a scrum to the other team.

Charge down

A charge down is not a knock-on. It occurs when a player blocks a kick from the opposition with their body. Even if the ball strikes their arm or hand and goes forwards, it is not a knock-on and play continues.

Left: Eyes on the ball, fingers extended.

Catching an awful pass or an awkward ball

In training, players should practise catching bad passes. Even so, in the match environment they still have to decide in each situation whether to catch the ball or leave it.

Drills
- *Throw the ball back and forth with a teammate catching it, getting progressively further apart.*
- *Get them to throw bad passes and judge whether to leave ones that are too far out of reach.*

A bad pass. Cory Jane has to break stride to leap to catch it.

A one-handed catch with the ball just within reach.

CATCHING A PASS

Preparing to catch a pass

Before the pass is made, catchers need to make sure they are in a good position to receive the ball. If they are unsure if the ball carrier is aware of them, they should make sure, usually with a shout. The receiver should be positioned, one, two or more paces behind the ball carrier, to run onto the pass.

Receiving the pass

The receiver should be looking at passer and ball, hands relaxed, fingers slightly splayed in front of their chest. If they keep their eye on the ball, the rest is instinctive. The fingers and hands will accept the ball and draw it into the protection of their chest.

Don't catch it with your chest

A mistake some players make is to catch the ball against their chest immediately. This can result in the ball hitting the chest first and bouncing off. The correct technique is to catch the ball with the hands and then pull it into the chest.

Missed pass or "hot potato"

There is one exception to not thinking before receiving the pass. That is when the receiver becomes aware that they will be tackled immediately and decides not to hold onto the pass. Instead, with a teammate outside them, they can either decide to let the ball go through to the teammate or help the ball on its way, by treating it like a "hot potato", finger-tipping it on immediately without holding onto it themself.

Drills
- One player runs ahead, the other follows behind, then comes left or right, calling for the pass.
- Running in a line, catch 50 passes in a row.
- Running in a line, attempt to catch various bad passes, leaving none.
- Running in a line, catch various bad passes, leaving those that will create a knock-on.

These drills will help you get a clear idea of what to catch and what to leave.

CATCHING A KICK

Golden rule — never let a rugby ball bounce

A rugby ball is an odd shape. There is no way of knowing which way it will go. Catch it in the air and you control it.

Catching from a kick

When catching a high ball from a kick, catchers must keep their eye on the ball. If they do this, they will automatically move towards the point where the ball will land, positioning themselves underneath it. If there are teammates nearby, the catcher must call loudly, such as "my ball", to tell them to keep out of the way. Positioned underneath the ball, the catcher spreads their arms like a basket to receive the ball. If they keep their eye on the ball, their arms will automatically close around the ball as it descends into the "basket" and automatically pull the ball safely against their chest as a secondary protection. Some coaches recommend a technique where the player holds their hands in the air, palms outwards, watching the ball descend through the triangle formed between the fingers. Choose whatever technique works best for you.

Quade Cooper prepares to catch the high ball, spreading his arms like a basket.

At least contest the ball to stop the other team getting it.   *Mark Cueto of England leaps high to make a clean take.*

Catching a contested kick

If the opposition is close by, then the catcher should jump for the ball for two reasons: one is to get higher than the opposition; the other is because the laws state that no player can be tackled in the air. The opposition has to wait for the catcher to get to the ground before they can tackle them.

Catching near the touchline

When they are near the touchline, players have to know exactly where the line is. If they have to glance down at it, they should do this as soon as the ball is kicked and thereafter keep their eyes on the ball. For a set kick, such as a penalty, one trick is for the catcher to step off the field of play so that the line is in front of them. Then they know exactly where it is and also have the option of jumping, catching the ball in the air and landing in the field of play.

Catching a kickoff or kick restart

Restarts are always competed, so the catcher, often the locks, should practise catching the ball with their arms extended above their head. If they wait for the ball to come lower, the opposition may well get to it first. This is also a skill that can be learned by a smaller player in any position, to give them an advantage in competing for the high ball.

Catching a wet ball

Practise with a soaked ball or one covered in soap.

> *Drills*
> - *Players kicking and catching standing six feet apart.*
> - *Repeat this, getting further apart and the ball getting high.*
> - *Catching with a jump.*
> - *Catching near the touchline.*
> - *The overhead catch.*
> - *Catching a wet ball.*

CONTROLLING THE BALL ON THE GROUND

Stopping a ball rolling or bobbling along the ground

If the ball is coming at a player in this way, rather than risk a knock-on, they should stop the ball soccer-style with their foot, then pick it up.

Picking up the ball off the ground

Players should also practise picking up a ball, stationary or moving, off the ground at speed by running forwards and scooping or snatching it up with one or both hands.

Falling on the ball

The loose ball can be secured by falling on it, but remember, rugby is a game played on the feet, so the player must immediately get back to their feet. This is often a good way to take control of the ball

when play has become scrappy. Ideally the defender falls on the ball, gathers it to their chest and springs back to their feet again in one fluid motion.

> *Drills*
> - *Stopping the ball with the foot.*
> - *Falling on the ball.*

Tonga's Viliami Ma'afu clutches the ball into the safety of his chest.

5 BASIC SKILLS — TACKLING

Tackling is one of the features that sets rugby apart from most other ball games because it is a full-contact game. In many ways it is the most challenging part of the game — a test of character and technique — but uniquely satisfying once mastered.

Tackling is vital to team defence as each individual tackle is the building block of the defensive pattern of the whole team.

TACKLING LAWS

A player can only tackle another who has the ball. The tackler cannot tackle early (before the player receives the ball); late (after the player has passed the ball); or when the player is in the air. The tackled player cannot be touched above the shoulders (high tackle). No form of striking is allowed, including using a "stiff arm". The tackler cannot tackle with the shoulder alone, but must use arms ("arms in the tackle"). The tackler cannot pick up the ball carrier and spear them towards the ground onto their head or shoulders (spear tackle).

ELEMENTS OF THE TACKLE

A tackle comprises five elements — courage, judgement, technique, timing, and the hit. The original meaning of the word "tackle" is to grab hold of the ropes that control the sails of a sailing ship. It is similar in rugby — to grab hold of your opponent and bring their progress to a halt. This then gives your team the opportunity to compete for the ball.

An effective tackle

An effective tackle halts the forward progress of the ball carrier.

A completed tackle

A tackle is complete when the opposing ball carrier has been taken to ground: they have at least one knee on the ground, are sitting on the ground or are supported by a player on the ground. The ball carrier has been taken out of the game and must release the ball.

A perfect tackle

A perfect tackle wins possession of the ball.

Above: A completed tackle because Wallaby Beau Robinson takes the ball carrier to ground.

Left: Alessandro Zanni of Italy has the ball. Stephen Jones of Wales wants it. Tackle!

Tackling mottos

- A player can't run without their legs.
- Tackling is all about body position.

KEY TACKLING SKILLS

Courage

Courage is inherent in everybody and is increased with success. Through a combination of correct technique and practise, a player learns that when tackling is done properly, there is nothing to fear. In the first instance, having the courage to tackle starts simply with the ability to look and see. The second is making the decision to make the tackle. If they have any doubt, the tackler must realize they have a responsibility to their team to make the tackle.

Judgement

The tackler must decide how to make the tackle. Tacklers should not look at the ball-carrier's eyes or face because they could be deceived: they should focus on the ball-carrier's body. The tackler will get an indication from the player's legs as to whether they might step or swerve. Likewise, the tackler will judge the ball-carrier's distance, speed and direction. The tackler will decide where to make the hit. The target area is between the knees and the chest. Maybe the player is big, so to bring him down the tackler needs to go low and take the ball carrier around the legs. Maybe the tackler wants to go higher to wrap up the ball. There might be a hundred or more factors with regard to the tackle and they might speed through the tackler's mind in a fraction of a second. After a lot of practise,

The tackler is well set to drive his shoulder into the ball carrier.

Perfect technique by Richard Kahui. Good driving body position and arms taking away the ball-carrier's legs.

tackling becomes instinctive.

Judgement also includes the decision of which type of tackle and what technique to use. These options are listed under Tackle Techniques, pages 60–63.

Timing

The tackler must decide when. Often this will be dictated by the ball carrier. They are the attacker and probably moving forwards. But if there is any way the tackler can dictate time and place, they should do so. This could involve: closing the gap, delaying until the ball carrier is more vulnerable, or "shepherding" them into a narrower space.

The hit — standard front-on tackle

The tackler accelerates or leans into the tackle, leading with one shoulder, placing their head to the side of the attacker's body, for their own safety, thrusting with their legs, leaning into the target area of the stomach with the full weight of their body, their arms enveloping the ball carrier. Ideally the tackler drives through the ball carrier, knocking them backwards and downwards, the tackler's hands and arms dropping behind the opponent's legs to pull at them in a counteraction to the driving shoulder so that the ball-carrier's body becomes

the victim of opposing forces. The ball carrier is effectively being cut in half and disconnected from the ground so that they lose their balance and topple like a felled tree.

Commitment & body position

Samoans are the best tacklers. They play like human torpedoes and understand that the keys to effective tackling are commitment and good body position. They often aim higher than the stomach, at the chest area, so this tackle is a slight variation on the previous one. Although going higher means the tackler won't be able to grip behind their opponent's legs, they should, at the moment of impact, be lower than the ball carrier and leaning towards them, almost off balance (if it were not for the counterweight of the ball carrier), rather like a person leaning forwards to push a heavy wheelbarrow up a slope. And the laws of physics tell us that the player with the lower centre of gravity will have the advantage; the ball carrier is usually higher (because they are holding the ball). The tackler tips forwards right to the edge of their balance and, with the final thrust of their legs, the full weight of their body goes into the tackle with maximum impact.

After the hit

In the modern game, there is an additional part to the tackle in that, after the hit, the tackler gets to their feet and competes for the ball.

Top left: Body position. Good angle from the tackler, so the ball carrier drops lower to counter it.

Middle: A low tackle that takes away the legs.

Left: A dangerous high tackle, such as this, would either be penalized or the offending player given a yellow card.

Right: Smaller Scotland back Phil Godman does enough to stop larger French forward Imanol Harinordoquy.

Low, straight and strong — All Black captain Richie McCaw takes on French captain Thierry Dusautoir in their 2011 Rugby World Cup match.

TACKLE TECHNIQUES

The front-on tackle

The most common tackle, as already discussed, is the front-on tackle, in which the ball carrier and tackler are facing each other. In theory, if both players are about the same size, moving towards each other at the same speed, the tackler should always win the contact.

The target areas

The three basic front-on tackle target areas are chest (higher), stomach (middle) and thighs (lower).

Accepting the tackle

A version of the front-on tackle where the tackler is stationary and the ball carrier is approaching at pace. The tackler then "accepts" the tackle, bracing for impact but not resisting it, getting a firm hold on the ball carrier and using the ball-carrier's own momentum to take them both to ground.

Low tackle

The target area is lower, from the hips to the thighs, with the purpose of taking their opponent around the legs and bringing them to ground. Often used by a smaller player on a bigger one.

Side-on tackle

The shoulder is thrust into the ball-carrier's hip. The arms go around the waist/hip area then slide down the attacker's legs, tightening around them, tripping the ball carrier.

Smother tackle

Another version of the front-on and side-on tackles is where the tackler goes higher to "wrap up" or "smother" the tackler's arms and the ball to prevent them from passing it. Here, there is less impact and more concentration on pinning the arms or the ball.

Tackle from behind

Very like the side-on tackle, except in this case the tackler targets the small of the back down to just below the buttocks and envelops the waist or hips with their arms.

The ankle tap

Tackle from behind in which the pursuer just reaches or taps the ball-carrier's ankles while they are running, knocking one of their ankles into the other and so tripping them up.

Below left: A tackle from behind by Canada's Sean Duke causes his Fijian opponent to spill the ball.

Below: A diving ankle tap by Kelly Brown of Scotland prevents France's Vincent Clerc from scoring.

Above: Nikki Walker of Scotland side tackles Ireland's Tommy Bowe.

Below: A big hit by Wallaby Pat McCabe puts Samoa's Maurie Fa'asavalu on his back.

Driving tackle

The ball carrier is upright and the tackler is at a higher angle so that with powerful leg drive they drive the ball carrier backwards several paces. To do this, it is necessary for the ball carrier to remain on their feet.

Touchline tackling

Close to the touchline, the tackler's intention is often to shepherd the ball carrier closer to the touchline and then drive, drag or push them over it to win the throw-in to the line out.

The half hold

Sometimes in match situations tacklers can only get half a hold or partly stop the ball carrier. This is acceptable if it stops the ball carrier long enough for them or one of their teammates to finish off the tackle.

Turning the player in the tackle

The ball carrier is turned to face the defending team to make it easier for them to win possession.

Drag-down tackle

The ball carrier is standing upright and stationary, and tacklers use their body weight to drag them down.

Leg pick-up

The ball carrier is upright and stationary, and the tackler lifts one of their legs to bring them off balance and tip them to the ground.

Gang tackling

Two or more players in the tackle against one opponent. A good tactic in junior rugby when there is an opposing player who is especially big for the age group.

Tackling the fend

When the ball carrier tries to fend off the tackler, the tackler has three options: go below the arm and use a powerful leg drive to break through the fend, to grab the fending arm and use it in a half hold to get in closer and make a proper tackle, or push the fend aside and then make the tackle.

The strip or rip

Sometimes defenders are able to get the ball from their opponent in the tackle. This is called "stripping the ball". They can do this with an arm or also aim for the ball with their shoulder when setting up the tackle and knock the ball loose from the ball-carrier's grip.

Tackling after a kick

Since players cannot be tackled in the air, opposing players must either compete for the ball in the air or wait for the catcher to land before tackling them. If the tackler times it right, they might hit them the moment the catcher's feet hit the ground.

Max Evans of Scotland lifts Wales' James Hook in the tackle and must bring him safely to ground.

The big hit

The one everybody likes to see! Usually more to do with timing than force when, as above, the tackler is able to arrive exactly as the attacker receives the ball, whether from a kick or pass, and has all their attention on it. Spectacular!

SELECTING & EXECUTING THE CORRECT TACKLE

Choose the technique that it is right for the situation. Sometimes players go for a big hit in open play and completely miss it! The whole idea is to stop the opposition and get the ball.

Get your first tackle in early

Like the first touch of the ball, the first tackle gets a person into the match. In the backs it is good to get a tackle in early on anyone you will be marking and to make sure it is a good one.

Crowding the ball carrier

Against a player who is exceptionally fast or tricky, try to get to them as soon as they get the ball, giving them no time or space to use their tricks or pace. Crowd them both as the individual marker and as a team.

Tackle strength

Though technique is the key, tackling is improved as a player adds strength.

Tackle practice

A team should spend a good proportion of the training session on defence. An amateur team should spend at least 50 per cent of it on individual tackling skills and team defence. The ratio is simple: the more time you spend defending in training, the less time you will spend defending in a match.

Excellent technique by Wallaby Luke Burgess, but Fiji's Waisea Luveniyall has his arms free to offload.

Dangerous tackle. The tackler was given the red card.

Drills

Every player should master every aspect of every tackling technique. Points can be awarded for "scoring" in many of these games to make them a contest (especially with children who will do anything if you make it a game).

- Evasion games like tag, also known as tiggy.
- Pursuit games like bullrush, also known as British bulldog.
- Touch rugby at walking pace.
- Touch rugby at running pace.
- Mirror image: two players face each other on either side of a line with cones set about 10 metres apart. The "attacking player" moves to the left or right. The defender tries to follow them and make a mirror image.
- Shepherding: in a grid with two players, who are not allowed to touch. One must shepherd the other into a corner until they cannot move.
- Block the tackler: in a grid, two players are not allowed to touch. The attacker seeks to get past the tackler who must get in the way to stop them.
- Block the tackler, contact: in a grid, the attacker seeks to get past the tackler who must get in the way and touch them with both hands to stop them.
- Hold the tackler: in a grid, the attacker tries to get past the tackler who must catch them and hold them for a count of three, with the attacker trying to get away.
- Wrestling: two players on their feet. One tries to wrestle the other to the ground; the other tries to stay on their feet.
- Pushing contest: each with their hands on the other's shoulders, two players try to push each other back.
- Body position: pushing contest between two players, one standing upright, and the other in proper tackle position.
- Body position: pushing contest between two players, shoulder to shoulder.
- Crowding: the ball is passed or kicked to the attacker. The defenders must arrive and touch the player before the attacker gets a chance to run.
- Tackling the catcher: one player jumps to catch the high ball; the other player times their run to touch the catcher, the moment their feet hit the ground.
- Practise all the above techniques with a teammate in slow motion and walking speed on mats or sand.
- Practise all the above techniques with a teammate, suitably padded, at jogging speed and full speed.
- Practise all of the above techniques with teammates in match-style situations, first in slow motion, then at walking speed, jogging speed and full speed.
- Make the situations more intense, reducing thinking time for the tackler until responses become instinctive.

Run, run! Hold on, hold on!

6 BASIC SKILLS — ATTITUDE

Attitude is how we look at the world around us. Your attitude to rugby is the ONLY thing that defines what you will get out of the game and how successful you will be in it. The same goes for your team. You should seek to learn and improve. Keep raising your standard and one day, maybe, you could play for your country.

DEFINING ELEMENTS

Professionalism

Even if you are not a paid rugby player, be professional. Turn up on time, be organized, be prepared, pay attention to the details and be the best that you can be.

Above: *Be confident. Be a leader. Be a competitor. Be a warrior within the rules.*

Left: *John Smit, a World Cup-winning captain for South Africa, exemplifies the right mix of resolve and respect.*

Confidence

Players gain confidence by knowing they have all the necessary skills, having learned and practised them thoroughly and to the best of their ability.

Competitiveness

A player should walk onto the field with the attitude that anything can happen and they are ready for anything. They should have a mix of confidence and alertness in equal measure. Overconfidence and overcaution alike will lead to defeat. If there are any nerves, they should use discipline and sense of purpose to overcome them.

Be a leader

Every team nominates a captain on the field. They are the only player who can consult with the referee and select options for penalties awarded during the match. Then the coach usually nominates a "pack leader" who leads the forwards. But there should be other leaders on the field. When England won the Rugby World Cup in 2003, several of their players on the field had previously been captains of the team. Anyone can be a leader. When the opportunity presents itself to lead in a situation, they simply have to take the responsibility.

Effort

Players should give the maximum effort at all times and make no excuses. Excuses are the songs that losers sing. When things go wrong, they should learn from it so they are better next time.

Enjoyment

If you are not enjoying it, you are doing something wrong. Find out what it is, fix it, and get the enjoyment back into your game.

Top: Both players are striving to do the best for themselves and their team.

Above: Prepare properly, including the warm-up.

Top right: Canadian and Japanese players shake hands following their world cup match in 2011.

Right: A tradition in Europe is to form a tunnel and applaud the opponents off.

Equipment

Equipment should be looked after. That includes rugby boots, a mouth guard (also called a gum shield), uniform, sports bag and any padding or other clothing or accessories used for the game. Kit should be prepared the night before a game and boots washed as soon as practicable after a game.

Respect the referee. Right or wrong, he's always right.

Health

Players should also look after their bodies by keeping fit and maintaining a balanced and healthy diet. Junk food and other unhealthy foods provide little energy. If you drink alcohol, be moderate with it — remember, technically, alcohol is a poison.

Treat your body as a temple and food as fuel. Eat foods that give you the most energy (not artificial sugars which give a false hyped-up energy "sugar rush"). Natural sugars occur in fruit, which are good recovery foods after training. Supplement your diet with multivitamins. Drink at least one nutritious protein drink a day. International players drink three a day. After a hard training session, the body muscle breaks down and you have half an hour to an hour to get the protein into the body to build it up again. A good formula, made in a liquidizer, is: 2 eggs, 1 tablespoon protein powder, 1 tablespoon brewer's yeast (rich in B vitamins), 1 teaspoon multivitamin powder, 1 teaspoon Spirulina, 1 tablespoon natural yogurt, and half a banana. Yum!

Referees

Players should remember that referees are human. If the players believe that the referee has made a mistake against them, then complaining only adds to the mistake. Treat it as a challenge to your own game to play better and make up for the referee's mistake.

Sportsmanship

Players should respect the opposition and play fairly against them but do everything they can during the match to beat them. After the match, win or lose, they should behave sportingly and develop friendships.

Right: The battle is over. Now the stories can begin.

7 SPECIALIZED SKILLS

There are two specialized skills that every player is capable of, though some use them more frequently than others. They are kicking and scoring.

KICKING

The fact that the leg is longer and stronger than the arm means the ball can be kicked further than it can be thrown. Kicking can gain long distances of territory (kicking for position) and is also a main method of scoring points.

Types of kicks in brief

Punt — ball kicked out of the hand.

Drop kick — ball is dropped from the hands and kicked as it rebounds off the ground.

Place kick — ball is placed on the ground and kicked from that position.

Hack kick — ball is loose on the ground and kicked (hacked).

The kick chase

There is a saying in rugby that a kick is only as good as the chase. The main chasers of a kick are usually the wingers, often first getting a signal from the kicker. Teams should work out systems for chasing a kick, with some players advancing in a line to compete for the ball or tackle receivers; others staying back to take the ball if it is kicked to them.

Dan Carter, all concentration as he kicks a penalty.

Gone with the wind

Nothing affects kicking as much as the wind. A strong wind at your back can act like an extra forward. Before a match, kickers should note how strongly the wind is blowing and in which direction(s); sometimes it swirls. One trick is to throw grass in the air and see which way it blows. Kickers must use a strong wind to their advantage while they have it because for the other half of the match, the other team will have it.

Kicking to touch

Any player is allowed to deliberately kick the ball off the field (but they are not allowed to throw the ball off the field). A line out is awarded to the opposing team, unless the kick was from a penalty kick.

Kicking indirectly to touch

If a player kicks the ball indirectly into touch, the throw-in is taken from where the ball went out. Indirectly means that before going into touch, it first touched the ground, a player or the referee. In this case, the kicker's team will gain ground from the kick.

Kicking directly to touch

If a player kicks the ball directly into touch, the throw-in is taken from level with where they kicked from (see exceptions below). Directly means the ball went straight out without touching anything first. The kicker's team gains no ground. This is also known as "going out on the full".

Kicking is a powerful weapon when used cleverly.

Kicking from the 22-metre zone

One of the special defensive rules that apply to the 22-metre zone is that if a defender kicks from it and the ball goes directly into touch the throw is taken from wherever the ball crosses the line. To be in the 22, a player needs to have only one foot on or behind the 22-metre line (25 yards). The kicker's team gains ground.

KICK FOR A REASON

Kicking should always be done for a reason. Generally, a team will kick more often the closer they are to their own goal line (and less the closer they are to the opposition's goal line).

Kicks fall into three basic categories, as shown in the diagram below:

A — a defensive kick to get the ball out of a team's own 22-metre line (25 yards);

B — a territorial kick from one's own half to get the ball into opposition territory;

C — an attacking kick, which is often used when in the opposition's half to try to get behind, or wide of, the defensive line.

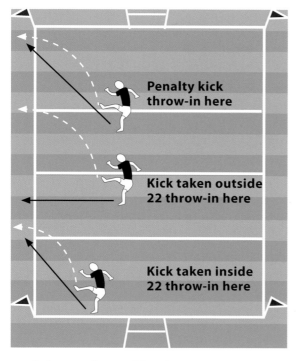

Penalty kick throw-in here

Kick taken outside 22 throw-in here

Kick taken inside 22 throw-in here

Golden rules of kicking · **kick for a reason · kick to space · kick accurately**

KICKING TYPES & TECHNIQUES

With all the following kicks, the non-kicking foot is planted on the ground, just prior to the swing of the kicking foot, to provide a firm base.

The punt

The punt is the most frequently used kick. The ball is kicked after being released from the kicker's hands into the air. The purposes of the punt are: to gain position and territory, and to put pressure on the opposition.

How to punt

The kicker tosses the ball a small distance into the air in front of them, drawing back the kicking foot behind the body then swinging it forwards, in time to strike the ball when it arrives below and in front of the knee of the non-kicking foot, so that the kicking leg is at maximum extension and will therefore generate the most power and distance. The ball is generally kicked through its middle at its widest part by the instep of the foot (the upper surface of the foot between the toes and the ankle). The head and shoulders are inclined forwards, and the eyes are fixed on the ball. The kicking foot strikes right through the ball, sending it forwards, the follow-through naturally aiming in the direction of the target.

The chip kick or chip-and-chase

A short punt is where the attacker chips the ball over the heads of the defenders. The attacker or a teammate then runs through the defensive line to chase the ball. The key to the chip kick is timing the kick so the defenders are setting to commit to a tackle, will be flat-footed and so slow to turn and give chase.

Jonny Wilkinson demonstrates the punt. Balance. Kicking foot back. Head down. Ball in front.

The grubber kick

A low punt with the ball bobbling along the ground. Like the chip kick, used to get behind the opposition.

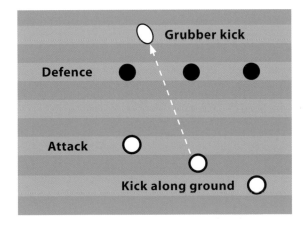

The wipers kick

An angled punt across the field in the direction of the corner flags. Perhaps named after the side-to-side motion of a windshield wiper, the wipers kick is used to change the direction of play and surprise the opposition. It is particularly effective when play has become massed on one side of the field and the opposition has little defence on the other side. In this situation, a wipers kick will often dribble into touch undefended, making good ground and setting the opposition back close to their own line.

The cross kick

Similar to the wipers kick, except it is very flat and always an attacking kick (while the wipers kick is often a territorial kick). The cross kick is best used when the attacking side has more players on one side of the field than the opposition has. The kick is made into space where unmarked players of the attacking side are waiting or can run on to it. Sometimes it is deliberately aimed for the attacking wing to catch out wide.

The screw or spiral kick

Kicking the side of the ball (similar to a spin pass) causes the ball to spin in flight. This reduces air resistance, allowing the ball to go farther through a flatter trajectory (the curved path of an object as it rises then starts to fall as gravity draws it down). The screw kick is effective when kicking to touch outside the 22-metre line when the ball needs to bounce first to get a territorial gain. The screw of the ball will to some degree reduce the irregularity of the bobble of a rugby ball so that the kicker can guide the ball into touch. It is also an effective kick to use when kicking into a strong wind.

The up-and-under kick or bomb

Also known as the Garryowen (after the Irish club that frequently used it), the idea is to kick the ball into opposition territory, high into the air "so it comes down with snow from the clouds on it", giving chasers time to get up and compete with or pressure the defenders. The up-and-under is a good tactic if the opposition fullback, or one of the

Drop kick. Note how upright the ball is . . .

. . . the kicker is well balanced with a nice straight follow-through.

wings, is a poor catcher of high balls. It is also very effective in rain. The ideal placement of an attacking up-and-under is usually just outside the opposition's 22, because if the ball goes into the 22 and they catch the ball they can call a "mark" or "fair catch". This means the opposition is not allowed to tackle the catcher. (The full rules for taking a mark will be given in chapter 10.) In a tight defensive game, the up-and-under is often used to pressure the opposition and force them to make a mistake. In a defensive situation, when the fullback, for example, is returning a kick and outnumbered, a safe option is to do an up-and-under over the heads of the opposition chasers.

The box kick

This is a specialized shorter up-and-under usually used by the scrum half (and sometimes the fly half) kicking from behind a scrum to a point directly behind it, targeting his blind-side winger sprinting forwards to catch it or compete for it. "Box" here is believed to mean that the kicker is kicking from one corner of a box, aiming for the opposite corner behind the opposition scrum.

The over-the-shoulder kick

A version of the box kick in which a scrum half, chasing backwards to collect a loose ball, has their back to the opposition and does a box kick over their shoulder before the opposition forwards can catch them in possession.

The drop kick

The drop kick is like a punt except the ball is dropped all the way to the ground and is then kicked at the instant that it rebounds. At the start, the ball is held vertically in both hands at about waist height. The kicker takes one or more steps forwards then drops the ball, pointed end downwards and tilted slightly backwards. The kicking foot is drawn backwards at the same time, and the foot swings forwards to strike through the ball with the instep, immediately after the ball has bounced off the ground. To get more distance, the kicker has a longer run-up and leans back more as they kick.

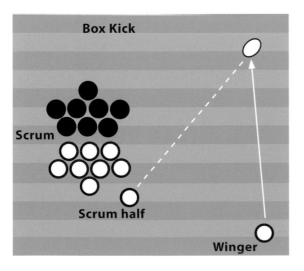

Drop goal. The ball is struck as it bounces up from the ground, here by Luciano Orquera of Italy with Irish players leaping to stop it.

The place kick

Most kickers place the ball on sand or a kicking tee and kick the ball with their instep. Every kicker has their own personal style, but it usually involves placing the ball and then taking measured steps away from it. Then they usually look at the posts, taking aim or visualizing the ball going through them. The kicker should be calm and relaxed and ignore any distractions. They usually take several steps towards the ball to build momentum, then the kicking leg swings through the ball and follows through in the direction of the target.

The hack kick

The ball is loose on the ground and opposing players are close by or the ball is difficult to pick up, so players can hack (kick) it forwards.

Drills

- *Watch rugby matches and award points from 0–10 for each kick in open play. Observe which kicks, executed in which way, are most effective in a match situation.*
- *Team kick chase.*
- *Hack kick — practise soccer dribbling (controlling the ball along the ground with the feet) with a rugby ball.*
- *Drop kicks from various positions, easiest to hardest.*
- *Penalty kicks from various positions, easiest to hardest.*
- *Punt tennis — similar to tennis, but using a volleyball net on grass, players punting and catching.*
- *Punt golf — kick towards an object to practise accuracy.*
- *Chip in the bucket — chip over a defender or obstacle of the same height at a bucket.*

- *Punt grids — players line up in a zigzag fashion on the halfway and one 10-metre line facing each other. They punt and catch the ball in a zigzag fashion from one end to the other, then do this at further distances back. Set up two sets of players doing this so they can race each other; the winner is the first to get the ball to the end of the line.*
- *All the types of punt kicks.*
- *Highest punt.*
- *Longest punt.*
- *Box kick — kick from the 22, aiming for a bucket on the 10-metre line.*
- *Aussie Rules Competitive one-on-one — two players stand one on each side of the field, punt the ball back and forth, forcing each other down the field; they must kick it from where they get it. The winner is the one who gets the ball over the opposition try line first.*
- *Aussie Rules Competitive in teams.*
- *Aussie Rules (version of) where the ball can only be passed by kicking and catching.*

Top right, from left: Jonny Wilkinson practises a goal kick: approach, head down; plant foot; kicking through the ball towards the posts.

Right: Note how Ronan O'Gara of Ireland attacks the ball in the final stride.

SCORING

It doesn't matter if you thought you played better than the opposition or "were unlucky" or "deserved to win", all that matters is that you scored more points than them by scoring tries, getting awarded a penalty try or kicking the ball over the goalposts.

Points' values

Try — 5 points
Penalty try — 5 points
Conversion — 2 points
Penalty goal — 3 points
Drop goal — 3 points

Scoring a try (5 points)

The law states: When attacking players are first to ground the ball in the opponents' in-goal, the attacking players score a try.

Getting over the line

Low body position will often get a player over a strongly defended goal line. If they are tackled short of the line, momentum might carry them over the line or they might be able to reach out for the line. In both cases, if they ground the ball, it is a try.

Scoring a try gives the team the right to take a kick at goal (conversion). When a player scores out wide, after they cross the line, they should run around closer to the posts, to make it easier for their kicker. Usually they should touch down before a defender gets close enough to tackle them.

Grounding the ball

Players should develop a secure technique for grounding the ball. Tries have sometimes been disallowed when a player "showboats" the finish or fumbles the ball. In a tight situation, they should

Try. A ball carrier short of the line, may reach out to ground the ball.

USEFUL DEFINITIONS & CLARIFICATIONS

GROUNDING

The law states there are two ways a player can ground the ball:

1. Player touches the ground with the ball. A player grounds the ball by holding the ball and touching the ground with it, in the in-goal. "Holding" means holding in the hand or hands, or in the arm or arms. No downwards pressure is required.
2. Player presses down on the ball. A player grounds the ball when it is on the ground in the in-goal and the player presses down on it with a hand or hands, arm or arms, or the front of the player's body from waist to neck inclusive.

GROUNDING AGAINST A GOALPOST

In addition to the goal line (try line), the post and padding are also part of the in-goal. If the attacking team is the first to ground the ball against a goalpost or padding (touching the ball against both ground and post or padding at the same time), a try is scored.

Note: Picking up the ball from the ground in the in-goal is NOT grounding it. You still have to touch it down, but can then do it anywhere elsewhere in the in-goal, such as running around behind the posts.

OFFSIDE DEFINED

Offside means a player being where they are not supposed to be, usually in front of the ball. However, a player in an offside position is usually not penalized unless they are interfering with play. At the start of a game all players are onside. As the game develops, players naturally get into offside positions. But don't worry, you won't get into any trouble as long as you don't interfere with play and take action to get onside.

THE OFFSIDE LINE

The offside line is an imaginary line which moves parallel to the goalposts. At the start of the match, the halfway line is the offside line. Then the offside line moves up and down the field, more or less following the ball, but varies for the different situations, such as scrum and line out, which are covered later in this book.

dive low to just get over the line, but they shouldn't aim for the line itself in case they are knocked back in the tackle. Aim just over it. Occasionally, in very wet weather, players have dived short of the line and managed to slide over it!

Preventing a try

In attempting to prevent a try, defenders are allowed to wrestle the ball free, but they are not allowed to kick it out of the ball-carrier's hands.

Scoring near the touchline

The ball has to be grounded before any part of the try-scorer's body touches the touchline (or anywhere beyond) or the ball will be "out". This skill should be practised by wingers and others who often score tries near the corner.

The ball carrier may touch the corner flag and can still score.

Dead-ball line

In the same way, in the in-goal, if a player, while putting the ball down, simultaneously contacts the touch-in-goal line or the dead-ball line, they are out. No try.

Corner flag

If the ball or a player carrying the ball touches a corner flag the ball is not out of play unless it is first grounded against a flag post.

Push-over try

A push-over try comes from a scrum in which the attacking team pushes their opponents over the goal line. Usually the number eight controls the ball with their feet, keeping it in the scrum until it is on or over the opponent's line, then they put a hand on the ball or fall on it to score the try.

Conversion (2 points)

A conversion can be a place kick or a drop kick. It is worth 2 points, so a converted try is worth 7 points.

Where to take a conversion from

A conversion is taken at a point in line with where the try was scored. If the try was scored under the posts, the kicker usually kicks from about 15 metres back. If the try was scored wider out, the kicker usually comes back over the 22-metre line to give themselves a better angle for the kick.

Placing the ball

Kickers must use the ball that was in play unless it is defective. They have one minute to take the kick, starting from the time they place the ball. They can make a mark in the ground, use a kicking tee, sand or sawdust. Even if the ball falls over in the wind, they still only have one minute. They can use a teammate as a placer to steady the ball.

Offside & charging the kicker

Except for the placer, all the kicker's team must be behind the ball when it is kicked or the referee will award a penalty to the other team for offside (see page 81 for a definition of offside). The defending team must go behind the goal line and are not allowed to charge until the kicker starts to run. The kicker and the placer are not allowed to do any trick that makes the opposition charge early. The defending team can charge when the kicker begins their run-up or begins to kick (if they have no run-up). So if the ball falls over after that, the ball is in play and the defenders can keep charging. In that case the kicker can kick the ball directly off the ground over the posts (if that's possible) or pick up the ball and drop-kick it. When charging (in any situation) the defenders are allowed to jump, but they are not allowed to support each other to stop the ball from crossing the crossbar.

Penalty kick (3 points)

The procedure for taking a penalty kick at goal is

the same as taking a conversion except there is no time limit and the defending team must stand at least 10 metres (11 yards) back and are not allowed to charge. But they have to remain alert because, unlike a conversion, if the kick misses and the ball stays in play, the game continues.

Defending the penalty kick

The defending team should have a set line-up to defend against a penalty kick with good catchers and kickers positioned behind and in front of the posts, in case the ball falls short or bounces back into play off the post or crossbar.

The penalty kick is successful

The ball is dead. The defending team has a kick restart at the halfway line.

The penalty kick is unsuccessful & the ball goes out

The ball is dead. The defending team has a kick restart from the 22-metre line — called a 22-metre dropout.

The penalty kick is unsuccessful & the ball is in

If the ball is caught in the in-goal by a defender or goes loose in the in-goal, the usual action is for a defender to touch the ball down. The defending team then gets a 22-metre dropout. However, if the defending team is behind on the scoreboard, with not much time left in the match, they may try to run the ball out from that position. If the defending team catches the ball in front of the posts, they have no choice but to play on.

Penalty try (5 points)

A penalty try is awarded by the referee when a defending team uses foul play to prevent what the referee considers would have been a certain try. The person who would have scored does not get the credit — the try is awarded to the team. The conversion attempt is then taken from in front of the posts.

Drop kick (3 points)

In open play, the ball is drop-kicked between the opponent's posts and over their crossbar. Drop kicks are a useful way of keeping your team's score ticking over in a close match. They are also a good way of winning a match in extra time. Two World Cup finals have been won that way.

> **Drills**
> - *Team defensive formation for a penalty kick.*
> - *Team defensive formation for a conversion.*
> - *Team defensive formation for a drop kick.*
> - *Scoring tries from various positions.*
> - *Grounding the ball — all aspects.*
> - *Scoring a try near the touchline.*

Penalty kicks are worth 3 points and can be vital in close matches.

8 SET PLAY — THE SCRUM

Set play or a "set piece" is a way of starting and restarting a game on the field. The game only stops when someone breaks the law; known as infringement. Major infringements, such as dangerous play, are punished with a penalty. On the field of play, after a minor infringement, such as a knock-on, play is restarted with a scrum.

WHAT IS A SCRUM?

A scrum is a pushing contest for the ball between opposing blunt-nosed battering rams, each consisting of a maximum of eight tightly bound players (usually the forwards). The ball gets put into the scrum by the non-offending side. Only the front-row forwards really know what happens in the front row of the scrum! The scrum takes place where the infringement occurred, but no closer than 5 metres to a goal line or a touchline. The referee marks the position with their foot.

The importance of scrums

Success or failure in the scrum affects the whole team. If one team's scrum is dominant, they will be going forwards and gaining heart; the other team will be going backwards, losing courage and tiring faster.

Why do scrums collapse?

Each front row in a scrum is desperately trying to gain an advantage over the other and sometimes one team deliberately collapses the scrum, or the pressures applied (also probably illegally) cause the scrum to collapse. Sometimes the referee can see who caused it, but often they can't.

BINDING

The whole arm, from hand to shoulder, must be used in binding to another player in a scrum. Just a hand on another player is not satisfactory binding.

The front row binds

The formation of the front row starts with the hooker in the middle. They raise their arms and may bind either over or under the arms of the props, gripping each by their jersey. In the same way, each prop puts their nearest arm around the back of the hooker so all three are tightly bound together.

Above: Head-on view of the Canterbury Crusaders' scrum.

Left: Bird's-eye view of the scrum. For England (white) the front row is 17, 16, 3; second row 19, 18; back row (obscured), 8, 6.

The second row binds

The second row lean forwards with the full extension of their body. Before they join with the front row, the second rowers bind with each other in a similar fashion to the front row — linking arms around each other's backs. The second-row forwards then place their innermost shoulder against the back of the hooker's thigh and their other shoulder against the back of the thigh of a prop. They grip the prop with their free hand. The reason why the second rowers are called "locks" is because all players other than the front row must bind (lock) on the body of one of the second row with at least one arm prior to the two scrums engaging.

The back row binds

A flanker may bind onto the scrum at any angle, provided they are properly bound. The two flankers place their inside shoulders against the outside buttocks of the two props. The flanker must not widen the angle so as obstruct the opposing scrum half moving forwards. The number eight puts their shoulders up against the buttocks of the two second-row forwards in front of them. Their arms go around their hips.

The scrum is ready to engage

Both scrums are formed up and bound. They are stationary and parallel, about an arm's length apart over the mark. At this point, the weight of the front row should be leaning slightly backwards to counter the weight of the second row and the back row behind them. The legs of the front row are splayed slightly outwards, their knees slightly bent, their backs straight. They look straight into the eyes of the opposing front row. They should be mentally prepared for the impact when the referee sets the scrum. Their intention is to move forwards, shoving the other team backwards. The ball is in the attacking scrum half's hands, ready to be thrown in.

Rear view of a scrum before engagement.

Crouch, touch, pause, engage

The referee calls "crouch" and the front rows crouch, each player's head and shoulders no lower than their hips. The referee calls "touch" and, using their outside arm, each prop touches the opposing prop's outside shoulder. The props withdraw their arms.

The referee calls "pause". There is a brief pause and then the referee calls "engage". This is not a command, but it tells the front rows they can now engage when ready. This might be varied in the future to stop scrums collapsing.

ENGAGEMENT

The front rows come together squarely with their heads interlocking so that no player's head is next to the head of a teammate. No player other than a prop may hold an opponent in the scrum. The prop's outside arm threads through the inside arm of the opposing prop and grips their jersey on their back or side; not on their arm, chest, sleeve, collar or anywhere else.

Staying bound

All of the front-row forwards must bind firmly and continuously until the scrum ends, though they can alter the binding within the law. All of the front-row forwards must have both feet on the ground, with their weight firmly on at least one foot. Players must not cross their feet. The hooker's foremost foot must not be in front of the foremost foot of their team's props. Players in the front row are not allowed to exert any downwards pressure. A team must not shove the scrum away from the mark before the ball is thrown in.

PUTTING THE BALL INTO THE SCRUM

The scrum half stands one metre from the mark on the middle line, holding the ball in both hands

Front rows touch.

Tonga and USA poised to engage.

parallel to the ground and touchline. When told to by the referee, the scrum half puts the ball into the scrum without delay and quickly in a single forward movement (no back movement is permitted). The ball goes into the middle of the tunnel so that it first touches the ground immediately beyond the width of the nearer prop's shoulders. The scrum half cannot pretend to throw the ball in.

THE SCRUM BEGINS

When the ball leaves the hands of the scrum half, play begins. Until the ball has left the scrum half's hands, the front row must not raise or advance a foot. As soon as the ball is in the tunnel, any front-row player may use either foot to strike for the ball (but not both at the same time). In practice, this is usually the hooker as the props have their feet planted on the ground pushing. If the ball goes right through the tunnel or comes out behind the foot of a far prop without being touched, the ball must be thrown in again. If the ball is unintentionally kicked out of the scrum, the scrum is retaken. If intentional, a penalty is awarded.

Winning the ball at the scrum

The players in the scrum should keep their backs straight and their legs slightly flexed, ready to push as soon as the scrum half puts the ball into the scrum. Scrum halves will often alert their own team by a coded call so they have advance warning. Strength, technique and courage decide who wins the scrum's pushing contest. As in tackling, the whole body should be aligned to give maximum push, the back remaining straight, all the forwards pushing as a single unit. The defensive scrum will try to disrupt the attacking scrum and push them off the ball.

The channels

When the ball has been won in the scrum, the forwards have to channel it to the back of the scrum where the scrum half or number eight can pick it up. No one else is allowed to touch the ball until it has been cleared from the scrum.

There are three basic channels. The first (channel 1) is between the prop and the left flanker. This is not a very safe option because the opposing scrum half will be hovering there, waiting to pounce. The safest channel (3) but most difficult to get to, is

Scrum half poised to put the ball in; his opposite beside him ready to compete.

between the second row back to the number eight who gets the ball on their right side so that their body will protect the ball from the opposing scrum half. In the middle channel (2) the ball comes to the left of the number eight.

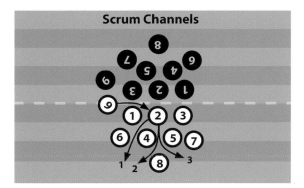

The player at left shows how the flanker binds on the side of the scrum.

Defensive flankers

As the ball is moving back through the attacking team's channel, the loose forwards of the defending team should raise their heads (though they still have to remain bound or they will be penalized) to see what the opposition is going to do with the ball. As the tight forwards cannot always see when the ball has come free of the scrum, one of their teammates who can see must shout to them to break when the ball comes out.

THE SCRUM ENDS

The scrum ends when:
• the ball comes out;
• the ball is at the hindmost player's feet (usually the number eight) who unbinds to pick it up;
• the ball is on or over the goal line and is grounded by an attacker or defender.

SCRUM VARIATIONS & OFFENCES

Front-row players must not twist or lower their bodies, or pull opponents, or do anything that is

likely to collapse the scrum, intentionally fall or kneel in a scrum; they must not lift or force an opponent up, handle the ball in the scrum or pick it up with their legs, or fall on the ball. Only front-row forwards can play the ball in the tunnel (not flankers). When out, the ball cannot be brought back into the scrum. A scrum half cannot kick the ball while it is in the scrum or make the opponents think the ball is out of the scrum when it isn't. A scrum half must not grasp an opposing flanker. If a scrum has to be reformed for any other reason not covered in the laws, the team who originally threw the ball in throws it in again.

Scrum collapse

If a scrum collapses or a player is lifted out of the scrum, the referee must blow the whistle immediately so that players stop pushing.

Wheeling of the scrum

If a scrum is wheeled through more than 90 degrees, a new scrum is set with the ball put in by the team that was not in possession when play was stopped. If no team had possession it is thrown in by the team that previously threw it in.

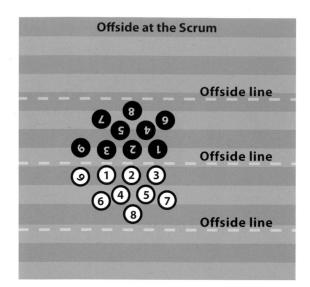

Offside at the Scrum

Offside line

Offside line

Offside line

Scrum halves offside at the scrum

Just before the ball is put into the scrum, everyone is onside. The two scrum halves are next to each other. The attacking one has the ball. The attacking scrum half is onside as long as they have one foot behind the ball. The defending scrum half is onside as long as they have both feet behind the ball.

The ball is put in. One team wins it. As the ball starts going back through the channel of that team, both scrum halves follow the ball. The attacking scrum half (of the team that has won the ball) is onside as long as they have only one foot in front of the ball.

The front rows have come up. This is illegal and will be penalized.

Defending scrum half offside

The defending scrum half is onside as long as they have no feet in front of the ball, or they can retreat from the scrum and stand behind the offside line which is set by the hindmost foot of their scrum. But they cannot go right around to the other side of the scrum because if they did they would go in front of the hindmost foot of the scrum on that side and that would now make them offside.

Offside players not in the scrum

The offside line for the other backs is 5 metres behind the hindmost foot of their scrum. However, if the hindmost foot is behind their goal line, the offside line is the goal line.

SCRUM PRACTICE

Scrummaging is VERY technical. Coaches should spend time ensuring players have their stance and body positions exactly right at the start. This is the best guarantee of safety and success. Only when the basic techniques are mastered can weight and opposition be added. If players have difficulty getting the exact angle right, one trick is to get them to push a car with the brake off. This will give them an idea of the direction of force required, because if they don't get it right, the car won't move.

> *Build your own scrum machine: this is a sled with padding for players to push and room on the back for other players to stand to provide weight and resistance.*
>
> ### *Drills*
> - *Basic techniques.*
> - *Pushing one-on-one.*
> - *Pushing front row versus front row.*
> - *Pushing with second row added.*
> - *Full scrum.*

The Bulls (blue) are defending and so their backs stand five metres back from the scrum.

Above: *Southland (maroon) push through and dominate the scrum.*
Below: *English Saxons decimate the USA scrum.*

9 SET PLAY — THE LINE OUT

The line out is the set way of restarting play for the minor infringement of the ball going off the field.

BALL IN TOUCH

When the ball leaves the field of play it is said to be *in touch*. To do this it must cross or touch the outside lines, or be carried by a player who touches one of the outside lines or the ground outside them.

The outside lines are the touchline, the touch-in-goal line and the dead-ball line (see the pitch marking and zones diagram page 21).

Keeping the ball in play

Even if the ball has crossed the line and not touched the ground, a player still standing in the field of play can reach over the line and catch the ball or knock it immediately back into the field of play.

When a ball has not crossed the line, a player off the field can kick or knock the ball back into play (but not hold it).

WHERE IS THE BALL THROWN IN FROM?

Usually at the point it left the field of play. This is called the line of touch. But if the ball goes out of play within 5 metres (5½ yards) of the goal line, the throw is taken at the 5-metre point.

Left: Jumpers, lifted by teammates, compete for the ball.

Left: The linesman lifts his flag to indicate where the ball went out.

Below: Flirting with the touchline. The attacker wants the ball to stay in, the defender (on the ground) wants it to go out.

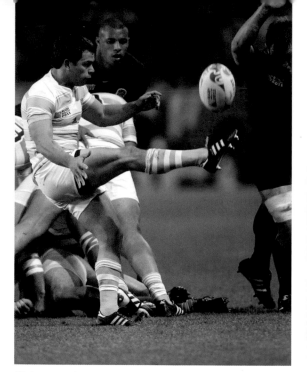

Kick to touch to improve your position on the field.

Todd Clever of the USA takes good clean ball in a line out against Russia in their 2011 Rugby World Cup pool match.

Kicking outside the 22

If the ball is kicked directly into touch outside a team's 22, the throw is taken level with where the kick was made (there is no gain in ground).

If it is kicked directly into touch from a penalty anywhere on the field, the throw is taken from where the ball leaves the field.

RULES FOR KICKING FROM THE 22 & GETTING THE GAIN

- To be in the 22, the kicker needs only one foot inside the 22 (which includes the line).
- The ball can't be passed back to them into the 22.
- The player cannot pick up the ball outside the 22 and retreat back into the 22.
- If the player is standing inside the 22 and leans over it to pick up a stationary ball the law says that they took the ball back into the 22.
- BUT if the player is standing inside the 22 and leans over it to pick up or catch a moving ball, the law says they can then kick the ball directly into touch.

The law if the ball is moving or stationary

This is a general law that applies in several similar situations. Essentially a player won't get in trouble if they are standing on or over a line and reach back across it to catch or pick up a moving ball (but they will if it is stationary). See the following example.

One foot in touch

The attacking team kicks outside their 22. The ball is going to land just inside the field of play near the touchline. But the defending winger knows the law. They stand with one foot off the field and catch the ball. That means the ball is now in touch. It has gone out on the full, so the line out takes place level with where the ball was kicked from and the catcher's team gets the throw-in. The catcher has won an advantage for their team.

FORMING A LINE OUT

Both teams form a line of players (usually the forwards) half a metre to each side of the line of touch as shown in the diagram. Therefore there is a metre gap between the two teams. The line out starts 5 metres (5½ yards) in from the touchline and finishes 15 metres (16½ yards) back from it. A receiver stands 2 metres behind each line. The thrower stands outside the touchline. One defending player stands 2 metres back from the line out and two metres in from the touchline (marking the thrower). These are the participating players. All other non-participating players (usually the backs) must stand at least 10 metres back from the line of touch, or on the goal line if that is closer.

Number of players in the line out

You need at least two players from each team in a line out. The team throwing in the ball decides the number. The defending team can have fewer, but not more. The attacking team does not have to announce the number. It is up to the defending team to count them. Once they have joined the line out, players cannot leave it until it has ended.

Jumpers & supports

The jumpers are usually the tallest players and stand at position numbers two, four and six, but this can be varied by the team throwing in. Usually the props stand at numbers one and three in the line out to support the main jumpers. The props, or whoever is next to the jumper, must protect the jumper from interference, assist the jump, and protect the ball from the other team.

Movement in the line out

Any player in the line out can stand in any position in the line out. Participating players may change places before the ball is thrown. The receiver

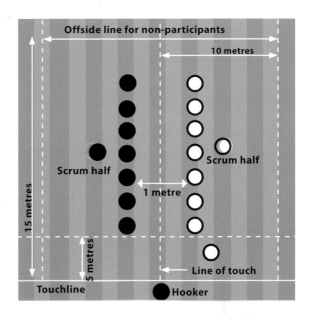

The perfect line out — accurate throw, high jump, two-handed take.

may run into the gap and perform any of the actions available to any other player in the line out. Depending on the defensive pattern a team uses, if the jumpers in the attacking team change position in the line out, so too will the jumpers marking them.

The shortened line out

This has no fewer than two and no more than six players on each side. Again the number is dictated by the team throwing in. They might choose shortened line outs because they have been losing a lot of normal line outs, they have a good jumper who will do better with more space, or they want to do a special move.

THE THROW-IN

Usually the team that was not the last to touch the ball before it left the field gets to throw it in. If that is not clear, the throw-in goes to the attacking team.

Top: Two lines form. The hooker must stand behind the line and throw accurately down the middle of the tunnel.

Middle: The code has alerted 4 of the attacking team (red) who prepares to jump, with 5 in support of him.

Left: The jumper has timed his attack of the ball perfectly to tower over his opponent.

From a penalty, the throw-in goes to the team that took the penalty (but not with a penalty kick at goal). From a free kick or a mark, the throw-in goes to the team that did not kick the ball.

Long throw-in

If the ball is thrown (often as a pre-planned move) beyond the 15-metre line (15 metres is about 16½ yards), a teammate may run forwards from behind the 10-metre offside line to catch it. An opponent can do the same.

Quick throw-in

A quick throw-in can be taken as soon as the ball has gone into touch by the team that has the right to the throw-in, but only if the thrower is the first to touch the ball, apart from the opponent who carried it into touch. If a player carrying the ball is forced into touch, that player must release the ball to an opposition player so that there can be a quick throw-in.

Opposition players are not allowed to prevent a quick throw-in. A quick throw-in cannot be taken after a line out has formed. The same ball must be used. The throw-in can be taken from anywhere between the place where the ball went into touch and the player's goal line. It does not have to be straight, but can also be thrown back towards that player's own goal line. The ball must travel at least 5 metres and the thrower must not step into the field of play when the ball is thrown. Opposition players are allowed to compete for the ball when thrown.

The throw

The player taking the throw-in (usually the hooker) stands behind the touchline and must not step into the field of play when the ball is thrown. The throw must be taken without delay, without pretending to throw, and travel at least 5 metres before touching

An accurate throw loops over the opposition's attempt to catch it.

the ground or a player. It must be thrown straight and travel through the channel between the two teams.

The code

The attacking team will signal to their own side with a code to warn them where the ball is going to be thrown. It might be a voice code such as the magic number code. For example, if 7 is the magic number, the number following will denote the jumper. So if the number called is "172", the jumper will be number 2. Or it might be a silent code, such as the scrum half putting one foot forwards (left = number 2 etc). There will also be a coded communication between the hooker and the jumper. Hookers can throw the ball flat or looped, quickly, delayed etc. They will signal their intentions to the jumper with their body language — twitches, raised eyebrows or even the way they stand — and jumpers might communicate in similar ways to indicate how they would like to receive the ball.

OFFSIDE IN THE LINE OUT

For participating players

Until the ball is thrown and has touched a player or the ground, the offside line for participating players is the line of touch. After that, the offside line is a line through the ball.

For non-participating players

For the players not taking part (usually the backs) the offside line is 10 metres behind the line of touch or their goal line, if that is nearer.

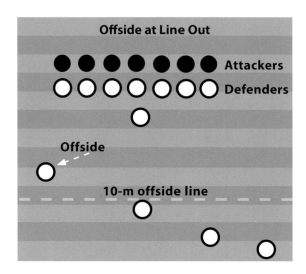

Offside at Line Out

●●●●●●● Attackers

○○○○○○○ Defenders

○

Offside

○

10-m offside line

○

○

○

Thrower offside

The line out begins as soon as the ball leaves the hands of the player throwing it in. Once the thrower has thrown the ball in the choices to stay onside are:

• they can stay within 5 metres of the touchline;
• join the line out;
• move into the receiver position if that position is empty;
• retire to the 10-metres offside line.

JUMPING IN THE LINE OUT

Players cannot jump before the ball is thrown and must jump for the ball, not into opposing players. But jumpers should assume they are going to at least collide shoulder-to-shoulder with opposition jumpers, so should jump aggressively for the ball.

There are three basic jumps:
1. they can jump forwards towards the ball;
2. jump straight into the air; or
3. jump leaning slightly backwards to take a looped throw from the hooker.

If there is space, the jumper can also take steps forwards or backwards.

Jumping infringements

Players in a line out can't lever off, hold, push, charge, block, obstruct or grasp an opponent. They can't cross the line of throw-in. If they do so accidentally while jumping, they must quickly get back to their own side.

Lifting

Players may lift and support a jumper, but not until they have jumped and not below the shorts from behind or below the thighs from the front. Pre-gripping is allowed.

CATCHING THE BALL

Ideally the jumper catches the ball in two hands. As soon as the ball has been won by a player of either team, the lifted jumper must be lowered to the ground. The props and other supporting players then bind on their teammate with the ball. The jumper should hold on to the ball until instructed to release it by the scrum half.

One-handed tap

The jumper can also tap the ball back with one hand as long as they use their inside arm. They cannot tap it back with the outside arm alone. But when holding the ball in two hands, either hand can be used to pass the ball to the receiver. An accurate tap-back gets the ball back to the scrum half quicker, who can then set up an immediate attack. However, a wild one-handed tap back that does not go straight to the scrum half often turns the advantage over to the opposition, who come chasing through after it. One-handed taps back are particularly dangerous in wet weather or near a team's own goal line.

Any player in the line out can catch the ball or tap it back.

A one-handed tap-back by All Black Brad Thorn.

Eyes on the ball, hands outstretched by England's Tom Croft.

DEFENDING A LINE OUT

Players in the defending team can try and crack the opposition code, jump for the ball, try to burst through any gaps in the attacking team's line out once the ball has been released, and generally try and put the opposition under pressure. The defending team's hooker should be marking the opposite hooker, alert for a blind-side move.

Defending teams sometimes choose not to compete (jump) in line outs, but wait for the other team to catch it and then try to push them back. This especially happens within 5 metres of their own line when the opposition forwards are likely to try and drive over the line.

MOVES FROM THE LINE OUT

The peel

A player may "peel off" (leave the line out) to catch the ball knocked or passed back by a teammate. They cannot leave until the ball has left the hands of the thrower and the player peeling off must keep moving until the line out has ended.

After the ball is thrown into the line out, the prop or another player peels off the front of the line out and runs back between the line out and the scrum half. The jumper, instead of passing the ball to the scrum half, passes or taps it to the prop, who makes a charge along the end of the line into the opposition forwards or backs. This is also known as the "Willie Away", named after Wilson Whineray, the New Zealand forward who invented it.

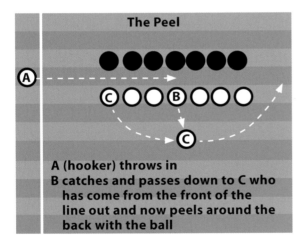

The Peel

A (hooker) throws in
B catches and passes down to C who has come from the front of the line out and now peels around the back with the ball

The blind-side charge

The hooker, after throwing the ball into the line out, stays on the blind side (the 5-metre gap between the front of the line out and the touchline). The ball is thrown back to the hooker (or another attacking player who moves to the blind side) by the jumper and the player charges through the blind-side gap, running down the touchline.

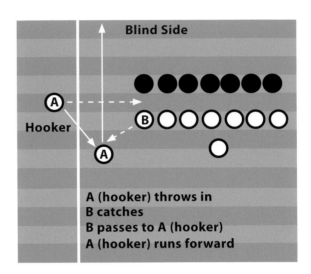

Blind Side

Hooker

A (hooker) throws in
B catches
B passes to A (hooker)
A (hooker) runs forward

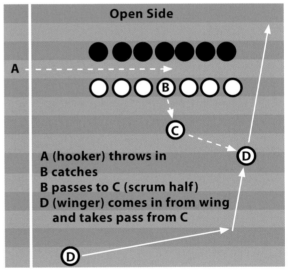

Open Side

A

A (hooker) throws in
B catches
B passes to C (scrum half)
D (winger) comes in from wing and takes pass from C

LINE-OUT PROBLEMS

If a line out is not started properly, the referee will get the same team to retake it.

If the line out is not executed properly, such as the ball not thrown in straight or not going 5 metres, the referee awards the non-offending team the choice of throwing in at a line out or a scrum on the 15-metre line (teams almost always choose the scrum because it is more secure possession).

Quick ball as it is thrown down to the scrum half.

LINE OUT BECOMES A RUCK OR MAUL

If the line out develops into a ruck or maul, then the offside line for players in the line out becomes the hindmost foot. The refs will often signal to the backs when this has occurred, which means they can move forwards to the new offside line.

LINE-OUT THROWING PRACTICE

Throwing the ball straight into the line out is one of the hardest skills to master in rugby. Like anything, it takes practise, and hookers should also practise in their own time. One way is to stand on the goal line and use one of the goalposts as a target. Mark or tie a target on the goalpost representing the hands of the jumpers, then pace back the throwing distance for each jumper, whether two, four or six in the line out. Get a friend to throw the ball back.

ENDING A LINE OUT

The line out ends when:
- the ball or a player carrying it leaves the line out;
- a line-out player hands the ball to a player who is peeling off;
- the ball is thrown, knocked or kicked out of the line out;
- the ball is thrown beyond the 15-metre line;
- a ruck or maul that developed from the line out leaves the line of touch;
- the ball becomes unplayable and play restarts with a scrum.

10 SET PLAY — STARTS, RESTARTS & ENDINGS

In addition to scrums and line outs, set play includes free kicks, penalties, restart kicks and kickoffs. So, let's get ready to start a game.

GETTING STARTED

The ground

According to the rules, you can play rugby anywhere, except on a hard surface. Grass is usual, but you can also play rugby on an artificial surface, sand and even snow, as long as the surface is safe. A team can object to the referee about the state of the ground or the way it is marked out before the match starts. The referee will try to resolve it. He must not start a match if any part of the ground is considered to be dangerous.

The referee's decision is final

The referee is the sole judge of fact and of law during a match. If no referee has been appointed, the two teams may agree upon a referee. If they cannot agree, the home team appoints a referee.

Touch judges & assistant referees

The ref might be assisted by a touch judge or assistant referee. A touch judge is responsible for

Perpignan prepare themselves physically and mentally before a quarter final of Europe's Heineken Cup.

signalling when the ball goes off the field. The assistant referee is a touch judge who is also trained as a referee and so can offer other assistance. If you sometimes function as a touch judge for your club, go to the International Rugby Board (IRB) website and read Law 6.4B through to 6.5B (it's only two pages) to see the signals you should use and what your duties are.

RUGBY GEAR

What you can wear

Players can wear a jersey, shorts, underwear, socks, rugby shoes, supports of elasticized or compressible materials (must be washable), shin guards, ankle supports (under the socks), mitts (fingerless gloves), shoulder pads, mouth guard, dental protector, approved headgear, bandages, dressings and thin tape. Women may wear chest pads.

Mouth guards

Players should definitely wear a mouth guard (also known as a gum shield) as this will protect the loss of teeth and other injuries. In junior rugby mouth guards are usually compulsory.

What you cannot wear

Players cannot wear anything with blood on it, anything sharp or abrasive, buckles, clips, rings, hinges, zippers, screws, bolts, rigid material or projections, jewellery such as rings or earrings, gloves, padded shorts, a single stud at the toe of the boot, and communication devices. So leave your phone in the changing room!

The referee or touch judges inspect the players' clothing before the match.

The warm-up

Players prepare in different ways. There was one international player who used to go to sleep until just before the kickoff, but most players will familiarize themselves with the ground, checking it out for anything unusual. They will do stretching exercises, being sure to warm up the body first with light exercise. Stretching should be done on a gentle gradient, gradually preparing the body for the rigours of the match. (After the match players should also do stretching exercises to warm down.) Players might throw a ball around to become familiar with it in their hands. The coach will no doubt give them a game plan and other advice.

The coin toss

The referee organizes the toss before the match. One of the captains tosses a coin and the other one calls it. The winner either chooses to kickoff or which end they will play from. The losing captain then gets the other option!

Going onto the field

Finally the team is ready to play and goes onto the field. Most players tune into game mode now, switching off all distractions, all their attention on the game.

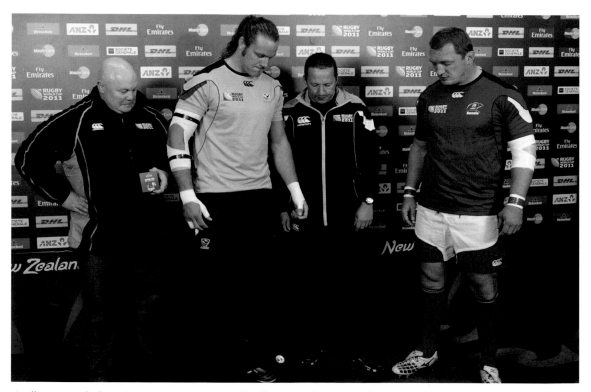

It all starts with the coin toss, a very serious affair between the USA and Russia.

INFRINGEMENTS & PENALTIES

But if we start playing under the laws, we are inevitably going to break them, so we first need to clearly define some terms.

INFRINGEMENT
An infringement is a breaking of the law, usually divided into minor (such as a forward pass) for which a scrum is awarded to the non-offending team and major (such as offside) for which a free kick or penalty might be awarded. An infringement is anything against the spirit of the game, unsporting or dangerous. It is not a matter of the intention of the act, but what was done.

FREE KICK
A lower-grade penalty which allows a team a free kick of the ball.

PENALTY
A higher-grade penalty which allows a team a free kick of the ball, including the right to take a penalty kick at goal and the right to kick the ball into touch and throw the ball into the line out.

THE KICKOFF
A kickoff is a drop kick at the start of each half of the match from the centre of the ground.

Restart kicks
A restart kick is a drop kick from the centre of the ground after a score or a touch down by the team that was scored against.

Lima Sopoaga of Wellington about to take a free kick.

Lining up for the kickoff
At the kickoff, all members of the team that is kicking off line up behind the kicker. The defending team will mark up against the attacking team. Their closest player must be behind the 10-metre line (11 yards) on their side of the field. Defenders positioned just behind the line have to be alert to the attacking team taking a "short" kickoff. In the area just behind that, the two defending locks will be waiting to jump for the ball, each with a prop next to them to lift and support them. The back row will be back behind them. The scrum half will be positioned nearby, ready to come forwards and receive the ball from whichever of his team wins it. The rest of the backs will be spread out across the field, the fullback in front of the goal line ready to take a long kick.

Where to kick

The kicker has to kick over the 10-metre line (11 yards). He places the ball and kicks to wherever was agreed by the team in the plan before the match. Usually all the forwards group to one side. Sometimes to deceive the opposition, the forwards are split half on the right and half on the left. Sometimes all the forwards are on the left, then the kicker kicks right in a pre-planned move to take the opposition by surprise. The rest of his team run behind him in a line before the kicker kicks and then pursues the ball. Various scenarios can occur from kickoffs and restart kicks and the following applies to both of them:

The kick does not go 10 metres

One of the defending team can elect to play the ball anyway. If they cross the 10-metre line and play it, the game continues.

Otherwise the referee gives a choice to the receiving team of awarding them a scrum at the centre circle or having the kick taken again (in practice, teams almost always choose the scrum because it gives them more certain possession of the ball in a better position).

If the ball crosses the 10-metre line but is blown back by the wind, that is okay — play on.

The kickoff goes directly into touch

The receiving team can elect to have:
- the ball kicked off again;
- a scrum at the centre;
- a throw-in from the halfway line (or behind it if the wind blew the ball back so it went off on the kicker's side of the field).

Beware: In this case the receiving team almost always chooses the scrum. Assuming this, the players of the offending team usually start to jog back to the centre circle, but sometimes the receiving team takes a quick line out catching them unawares. Tries have been scored in this way.

The kick goes directly into the opposition's in-goal area

If the ball goes out or the defending team grounds the ball, a free kick is awarded to the defending team at the centre of the halfway line.

> **Drills**
> - *Various attacking kickoff options.*
> - *Various defensive kickoff options.*

DEFENSIVE TOUCH DOWN

Touch down defined

A touch down is the opposite of a try. A defending team touches the ball down in their own in-goal. The law states: When defending players are first to ground the ball in the in-goal, the defending players make a touch down. The ball is then dead, preventing an attacking team scoring.

Grounding a touch down

Exactly the same rules apply as for a try (see page 81): held in the hands and arms or downwards pressure anywhere on the front of the body from waist to neck.

Attacker sends ball into in-goal

If an attacker sends or carries the ball into the opponent's in-goal and the ball is grounded by a defender, a dropout is awarded to the defending team.

In general play, if the attacking team kicks the ball so that it goes out of play in the opponent's

The kickoff with all players behind the kicker. Now they must pursue the ball.

in-goal (not from a penalty kick or a drop goal attempt), the defending team can choose to have a dropout or a scrum from where the ball was kicked.

Carried back

If a defending player takes (carries, kicks or knocks) the ball back into the in-goal and grounds it, a 5-metre scrum (scrum at the 5-metre line — about 5½ yards) is awarded to the attacking team.

Doubt about grounding

If there is doubt about who grounded the ball, play is restarted with a 5-metre scrum awarded to the attacking team.

22-METRE DROPOUTS

Dropout from the 22-metre (25-yard) line

The dropout is similar to the kickoff or restart from the halfway line, but taken in the 22, as shown in the diagram. At least one member of the opposing team (player A in diagram opposite) will try to obstruct the kicker (player B) or charge down the ball, but they are not allowed to cross the 22-metre line.

Options for the 22-metre (25-yard) dropout

The usual tactics are to drop-kick the ball high into the air for the kicking team's forwards to jump for, or to kick long into the opposition half, the option taken by the kicker in the diagram. Sometimes teams do tricky little dropouts to try to win back possession of the ball — such as the kicker kicking it only just over the line, along the ground, to a teammate standing close by — but these moves are riskier than the long kick.

The dropout does not cross the 22-metre line

If the ball does not cross the 22-metre line and the opposing team gets an advantage, it is play on. Any opponent who plays the ball can score a try.

If there is no advantage, the opposing team has a choice of another dropout or a scrum at the centre of the 22-metre line.

The dropout is kicked directly into touch

The opposing team has three choices.
1. They are awarded a scrum at the centre of the 22-metre line and they get the put-in.
2. They can accept the kick, in which case a line out takes place and they get the throw-in.
3. They can have the dropout retaken.

The dropout goes into the opponents' in-goal

This would take a long kick, probably wind-assisted, but if it happens, the defending team can play on. Or they can ground the ball or make it dead, in which case they have a choice of having the dropout retaken, or a scrum with put-in at the centre of the 22-metre line from where the kick was taken. They would probably likely choose the latter because it offers them both possession and position.

Offside at the 22-metre dropout

All the kicker's team must be behind the ball when it is kicked. If not, the non-kicking team is awarded a scrum at the centre of the 22-metre line.

However, if the kick is taken quickly so that players of the kicker's team are retiring and still in front of the ball, they will not be penalized as long as they try to get onside.

Drill
Various 22-metre dropout options.

HALF-TIME

A full 40 minutes has been played and it is now half-time. The players change ends or can leave the field, get some refreshment and get their half-time telling-off from the coach. The half-time interval can last no more than 15 minutes. When the players come back on the field, the team that received the kickoff at the start of the match now kicks off.

CALLING A MARK

Calling a mark or fair catch

The attacking team kicks the ball back into the opposing 22 where the other special defensive rule comes into play. It is that inside the 22-metre area, in open play, a defender can make a clean catch of a ball kicked into the air by an opponent and claim a "fair catch" or "mark". To do this, they simply call "mark" as they catch the ball, loud enough for the referee to hear. The referee will then blow their whistle to stop opposition players tackling the catcher. But the catcher should keep playing until they hear the whistle, in case the referee does not hear his call. If he does, the referee will award the player a free kick.

Rules for calling a mark

The catcher only needs one foot on the 22-metre line to call a mark. A mark cannot be made from a kickoff or a restart kick except for a dropout. The mark can be called even when the ball has first touched a goalpost or the crossbar. Any defender can take a mark in the in-goal.

Rules for kicking a mark

The kick is taken by the player from where they made the mark (but at least 5 metres in from the touchline). The opposition must not charge as the kick is being taken. The catcher may take a tap kick and run, or take a tap kick and pass to a teammate who kicks (the opposition can immediately charge the teammate). If the ball is kicked directly to touch from a mark, the opposition will get the throw-in.

Drill
• *Taking a mark.*

FREE KICKS & PENALTIES

Where is a free kick or penalty taken from?

At the place of infringement, as indicated by the referee or from any place in a line behind it, though not within 5 metres of an opponent's goal line or touchline. The opposition must immediately retreat 10 metres and allow the attacking team a "free kick" of the ball, though they can charge as soon as the kicker starts his run or kicks.

If a penalty is awarded to a team after they have kicked the ball in general play (such as for a late charge on the kicker) it is awarded wherever the ball lands.

Taking the kick

A free kick or penalty should be taken without undue delay. Any player can take one with any type of kick: punt, drop kick or place kick, with any part of the lower leg from knee to the foot, but not including the knee and the heel.

A player can punt or drop-kick a ball to touch, but not place-kick it. After having kicked the ball the kicker is allowed to immediately play the ball again, without another player having touched it. Any infringement from the defending team and the referee advances the original free kick or penalty 10 metres.

Differences between free kicks & penalties

• With a free kick the defending team can charge the kicker; with a penalty they can't.
• With a free kick if you kick the ball directly into touch, you don't get the throw-in to the line out; with a penalty you do.
• With a free kick you can't take a place kick at goal; with a penalty you can.

Referee signals

• The referee signifies a free kick by raising his arm bent.
• The referee signifies a penalty by raising his arm straight.

No drop kick after free kick

To stop players simply taking a quick tap penalty (see next) and passing it to a teammate who takes a drop kick at goal, the law states, you can't take a drop kick immediately after a free kick. Before you take a drop kick, one of your players has to be tackled; or one of the opposition has to have touched the ball; or the ball has gone dead.

In some cases, the referee will give the option of a free kick or a scrum. If the scrum is chosen, this rule still applies.

THE TAP KICK OR TAP PENALTY

When a team has been awarded a free kick or a penalty kick, one option is to take a quick tap kick. The kicker taps (lightly kicks) the ball up into their own arms and then can play on. This is a very good option for a free kick if the opposing team is not ready to defend. If they tackle the player within 10 metres of the mark they will concede a full penalty and this one may be within kicking range of the posts. Otherwise, if there is space ahead or if the attacking team has players in support, by taking a quick tap kick, they might be able to mount an attack that reaches deep into opposition territory.

But they have to take the kick from the correct mark. If not, the referee will call it back, which happens frequently. Players taking the tap penalty have to either be certain where the mark is or they have to ask the referee.

Defending against tap penalties

Once a referee has awarded a free kick or penalty, a frequent mistake made by the defending team is to drop their heads in disappointment, lose their concentration or even turn their backs on the opposition as they troop back the regulation 10 metres (11 yards). Even though the referee has blown the whistle, the game has not necessarily stopped. Defenders have to be alert to the tap kick, though they are not allowed to do anything to prevent it being taken quickly. Even after the kick is taken, players who are offside still have to retire the 10 metres before they can participate in the play.

Defending against the forward charge

A team will often use a tap penalty to start a forward charge. To counter this, the defending forwards should face up to the tap penalty in a line about an arm's width apart, the strongest tacklers in the middle. If the offside line is the goal line, the defenders have to charge forwards as soon as the tap penalty is taken, otherwise the attackers' momentum will take them over the line.

Penalty kick at goal

Once an attacking team indicates they will take a penalty kick at goal, they can't change their minds or do something else like take a tap penalty. The defending team must stand still with their hands by their sides from the time the kicker starts to approach to kick until the ball is kicked.

> ### Drills
> • *Defending against a tap penalty.*
> • *Defending against a penalty that misses.*
> • *Defending against a penalty that hits the posts or falls short.*

INFRINGEMENTS

Offences & allowances

A player cannot: punch, strike, kick, stamp, trample, trip or retaliate (strike an opponent because they have broken the law). They can't push, hold, obstruct or block a player when they don't have the ball (except in a scrum, ruck or maul); charge them when the player charging is not the ball carrier, waste time, throw the ball into touch.

A player is allowed to: tackle as hard as they like within the rules, charge at opposing players as hard as they like when the charger is the ball carrier, kick the ball into touch.

Sins & seeing red

In addition to a free kick or a penalty against them, offenders can be cautioned (warned); sin binned (yellow card — 10 minutes off the field); or sent off for the rest of the match (red card). Repeated infringements by the same team might lead to a warning followed by the next offender being sin binned. If repeated, the next offender gets sent off.

Penalty kick. The defenders are at least 10 metres back and spread out to catch the ball if it misses.

Offside in general play

Accidental offside

When players in an offside position are touched by the ball or a teammate carrying the ball they are accidentally offside. If the player's team gains no advantage from this, play continues. If the player's team gains an advantage, a scrum is awarded to the opposing team.

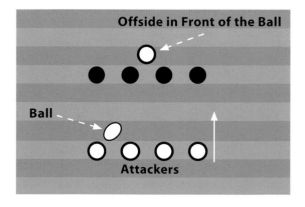

Offside preventing an advantage

However, when a player knocks on and an offside teammate plays the ball next, the offside player is penalized if he prevented an opponent from gaining an advantage.

Offside from a kick in general play

When a player in an attacking team kicks the ball forwards, any attacking player in front of him is offside. There are several ways in which an offside player can quickly get onside, as shown in these diagrams at right, and on the previous page.

• The offside player can run behind the ball carrier (1).

• The ball carrier can run in front of the offside player (2).

• The kicker can run in front of the offside teammate, or a teammate who is level with or behind the kicker can run in front of the offside player (3).

• An opponent who is carrying the ball may run 5 metres (5½ yards) (4).

• An opponent may kick or pass the ball (5).

• An opponent may intentionally touch the ball but not catch it (6).

Offside under the 10-metre law

When a player (A in the diagram) kicks the ball up field, any teammate in front of them (B, C and D) must be at least 10 metres (11 yards) back from where the ball lands. If they are within 10 metres, they must retire to this imaginary line or they will be offside. However, they can be put onside if a teammate who started running from an onside position draws level with them. The offside rule still applies even if the ball has hit a goalpost or a crossbar. What matters is where the ball lands. The 10-metre law does not apply when an offside player gets the ball as a result of an opponent charging down the kick.

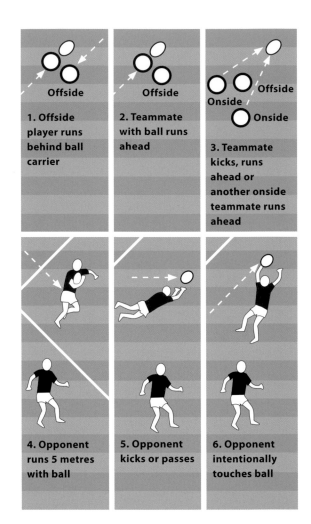

1. Offside player runs behind ball carrier

2. Teammate with ball runs ahead

3. Teammate kicks, runs ahead or another onside teammate runs ahead

4. Opponent runs 5 metres with ball

5. Opponent kicks or passes

6. Opponent intentionally touches ball

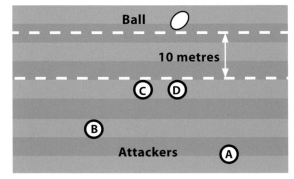

Loitering

A player can be penalized for loitering in an offside position.

- *Imaginary offside line — lay a pencil on the diagram of the field of play and move it up and down, following an imaginary offside line.*
- *Imaginary offside line — on the actual field, players follow the ball as it moves all over the field and staying in a line behind it.*
- *Offside in front of the ball — player offside and teammate knocks on, player practises leaving the ball.*
- *Getting onside by running behind the ball carrier.*
- *The ball carrier running in front of the offside player.*
- *The kicker running in front of the offside teammate.*
- *Teammate who is level with or behind the kicker running in front of the offside player. Opponent who is carrying the ball running 5 metres (5½ yards).*
- *An opponent kicking or passing the ball.*
- *An opponent intentionally touching the ball but not catching it.*
- *Getting onside under the 10-metre law.*
- *Put players in various offside positions (without telling them what they are) and tell them to get onside.*
- *14 against 15 playing with a man short who has been sent to the sin bin.*
- *13 against 15 playing with two men short who have been sent to the sin bin.*

END OF THE MATCH

How long does a match last?

A match lasts 80 minutes of actual playing time. In hot conditions, the ref can also order one drinks break per half. Extra time may be played such as in a knockout competition. Any stoppages in a match are added on at the end.

When does a match end?

When the ball next goes dead after the 80 minutes are up. But the ref allows more time for a conversion to take place and to complete a mark, free kick, penalty, scrum or line out already awarded. The next time the ball goes dead after these, the match is over (but if there is a collapsed scrum, the scrum is retaken).

The referee blows the whistle for the end of the match. One team celebrates, the other shakes their heads, then both come together in honour, respect and the comradeship of rugby.

Drills

- *Match endings — set up various scenarios and get the players to say if the match can end or not.*
- *Continue playing after the 80 minutes with the whole team keeping the ball alive after time is up.*
- *The handshake or hug at the end of the match.*

11 PHASE PLAY — TACKLE, RUCK & MAUL

Rugby has set play, open play and phase play. Set play starts and restarts a game. Open play is when the game is flowing. Phase play is when open play is interrupted by tackles, rucks and mauls (collectively known as "the breakdown"). It is when play pauses and starts on its own (without the referee having to blow their whistle). This is the most contested part of the game on the field and generally the least understood. Of course when you do understand it, as you are about to, it is very simple.

PHASE DEFINED

The normal meaning of phase is a stage in a process. In rugby a phase is one contest of the ball followed by one period of open play.

Examples of phase play

Scrum half passes back from scrum. We have now left set play and are in open play. Centre charges forwards with the ball. Gets tackled (phase 1 begins). Maul. Ball comes out and is passed to winger (phase 1 ends). Winger tackled and brought to ground. Ruck forms. Attacking team keeps possession and throws the ball out again. Pass after pass. Player held but manages to offload (phase 2).

The contest for the ball is the essence of phase play.

Next player tackled. Ruck. Ball comes out on same side again. Forward picks it up and drives (phase 3). A maul develops, this collapses accidentally, ruck forms (maul and ruck continuous). Attacking team win it and pass the ball out again. They attack again (phase 4), but throw the ball forwards. Scrum (set play). End of phase play. The attacking team held the ball for four phases.

Tackle, ruck & maul defined

- Tackle is a contest where the ball carrier is stopped by an opposing player.
- Ruck is a contest where one or more players from each team are trying to push their opponents off the ball which is on the ground.
- Maul is a contest where at least three players (at least one from each team) are competing for the ball which is in the hand.

Got it? Ruck = ground; maul = hand.

Examples:
- Two opposing players on their feet wrestling for the ball — tackle.
- A third player joins them and wrestles for the ball — maul.
- The ball goes to ground and now they try to push each other off it — ruck.

Gain line

Part of the theory of phase play is crossing the gain line. This is the imaginary line between the opposing forwards that the ball carrier has to cross to make a forward advance. As long as a team in possession keeps crossing the gain line, in theory, they would eventually cross the try line.

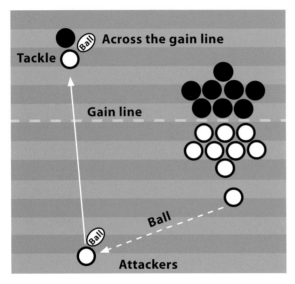

Holding onto the ball

Keeping possession of the ball is one of the keys to winning rugby matches. While attempting to score, a team wants to keep possession of the ball for as many phases as possible until they score.

Deliberately setting up a ruck or a maul

In the modern game, teams deliberately set up rucks and mauls to tire and draw in opposition defenders. As the defenders are concentrated in close, that creates more space wider, giving more opportunity to score. Attackers try and set up the ruck or maul by the simple and primitive action of their ball carrier smashing into the defensive line with teammates in close support.

Drills
- *Get each player to explain the basic difference between a ruck and a maul.*
- *Get each player to explain phase play.*

Attacker and defenders will try to set up a ruck or a maul to their own advantage.

If he stays on his feet a maul may form. If the ball goes to ground it's a ruck.

A ruck has not formed over the ball so Cory Jane is able to pick it up.

TACKLED BALL

A tackle is started when the ball carrier is stopped by an opponent. It is finished when the tackler takes the ball from the ball carrier, the ball carrier is brought to the ground, a ruck or maul is formed, or the referee blows for an infringement.

Taking the tackle

The ball carrier is about to be tackled. They can't pass it, there is no teammate available in support, so they elect to take the tackle. Now they are trying to control it so that it occurs to the advantage of their team.

Setting up the next phase

The first decision to be made is whether to attempt to stay upright and form a maul or go to the ground and form a ruck. The ball carrier should never go to ground if there is no support close by, as opposing players on their feet will have the right to play the ball and the ball carrier won't. In this case the ball carrier tries to stay on their feet until help arrives.

Staying on the feet

The ball carrier shields the ball from the opposition, twisting their body to present the ball back to their own team and use their own body as a shield.

Tackled player goes to ground

The ball carrier might go to ground either by choice or because they have no choice.

Definition of "brought to ground"

The ball carrier has at least one knee on the ground or is sitting on the ground, or on top of another player on the ground.

Tackled player protects the ball

As in the maul, the player turns their body towards their own goal line to shield the ball from the opposition. When tackled players are brought to the ground and are held in the tackle, they must pass, place, push or release the ball immediately.

The tackler must release

The tackler is off their feet and must release the tackled player. The tackler has a choice of either rolling away to allow the game to continue or get to their feet to challenge for the ball. The tackler must not illegally prevent the other team from getting the ball. Nor can the tackler tackle or attempt to tackle an opponent while the tackler is on the ground. Only players on their feet have rights. However, the tackler does have the right to immediately get to their feet and compete for the ball. They must be on both feet, not one foot and one knee.

In-goal exception

If the ball is loose, any player who is off their feet can dive on the ball and score a try or make a touch down.

The ball carrier places the ball

The ball-carrier's rights to the ball are almost at an end, but they usually seem to manage to make "immediately" last a second or two longer. If they are not held they can release the ball, get up, pick it up and start running again.

The tackler competes

The tackler has got to their feet and is competing for the ball. Now the ball carrier must release it or they will get penalized. They release and the tackler rips the ball away and passes it to a teammate.

Turnovers

When one team wins possession of the ball, it is called a turnover. A good loose forward may win several turnovers at the breakdown in a match.

Main problems at tackled ball

- Ball carrier holds on too long.
- Tackler does not get to their feet before trying to play the ball.
- Tackler gets to their feet, but goes off their feet again when competing.
- Tackler or new players are knocked off their feet by new players arriving.
- New players arriving go off their feet.
- Players lie on the ball or in a position to make it unplayable.

Ball unplayable

If new players enter the contact area and the ball becomes unplayable or the situation becomes dangerous, the referee awards a scrum with the throw-in to the team that was moving forwards. If no team was, then it is awarded to the attacking team.

The contest escalates as more players join it. Now we have a ruck or a maul. But which is it?

Drills
- *Ball carrier deciding to take the tackle.*
- *How long can a player stay on their feet in the tackle as the opponent tries to drag them down. Practise without and then with the ball.*
- *Going to ground and protecting the ball.*
- *Passing the ball out of the tackle.*
- *Passing the ball immediately from the ground.*
- *Placing the ball; then pushing it away.*
- *Releasing the ball, getting to the feet and picking it up again.*
- *Tackler on feet competing for the ball; and then competing while retaining balance despite buffeting from opposition and teammates.*

RUCK

What's the difference between a ruck and maul? With a maul, the players are on their feet and the ball is in the hand. With a ruck, the players are on their feet and the ball is on the ground.

A ruck is formed when at least two opposing players are in contact with each other over a loose ball on the ground. As players form or join a ruck they must bind on a teammate or an opponent, using the whole arm. With short pumping steps, they attempt to step over the player and the ball and drive back any players opposing them. Stepping over the ball and driving forwards is known as "blowing over". The trick is to get more teammates there before the opposition and outnumber them early. Sometimes the ball becomes stuck in the ruck behind bodies that are in the way and an attacking team needs to dig the ball out with their feet. This has to be done carefully so as not to injure any players lying on the ground, as referees will award a penalty for anything that looks like dangerous play.

Ruck defined

A ruck has at least one player from each team, on their feet, in physical contact, competing for the ball on the ground, trying to step over it and push their opponents off it. A ruck is an impromptu scrum. If the ball is off the ground for any reason, it is not a ruck.

Offside at ruck (& maul)

A player joining a ruck or maul must do so from behind the foot of their hindmost teammate in the ruck or maul. Players must either join the ruck or maul or retire behind it. They cannot loiter at the side of it. Any player not in the ruck or maul should be behind the back foot. If that is behind their goal line, the offside line is the goal line.

Backs in the ruck & maul

When a tackle is made in the back line and the forwards are slow to arrive, the nearest backs must engage in the ruck or maul.

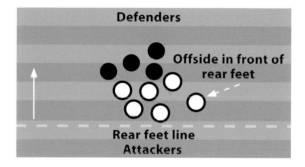

Not joining a ruck

If the first wave of forwards has control of the ruck, then players arriving late should not enter the ruck but position themselves just behind it, waiting to see what develops.

HISTORICAL RUCK

The ruck was invented by Vic Cavanagh, coach of Otago in New Zealand in the 1940s. He organized his forwards into a loose scrum but bound so tightly together that you could "throw a blanket over them". They drove over the ball on the ground, blasting the opposition off it and giving his side quick ball. That is one of the main advantages of a ruck — quick attacking ball before the opposition can regroup.

LAWS THAT GOVERN BOTH RUCK & MAUL

New players arriving at the breakdown, whether it is a ruck or a maul, must enter from the rear. Think of a ruck or maul as being like a small sheep pen. Those that want to join it must enter through the gate at the back. They must bind with the players who are already a part of it. Their heads and shoulders must be no lower than their hips. Players who are not in the ruck or maul should be behind the hindmost foot in the ruck or maul, or they will be offside.

Ruck restrictions

- The ball cannot be picked up with the hands or the feet.
- Once the ball has left a ruck, it cannot be pulled back into it.
- Players must not deceive the opposition that the ball is out of the ruck when it isn't.
- Players cannot be rucked or stepped on when lying on the ground.
- A player cannot jump on a ruck or collapse a ruck.

Clearing a ruck

Because ruck ball is meant to be fast, the ball has to be cleared fast or the advantage will be lost. That means the nearest player often has to jump in as scrum half. Sometimes the ball will be popped up to forwards waiting to charge forwards and set up the next ruck. If the opposition forwards are out of position, a series of rucks can be continued in this way down the field.

Pick-and-go

Pick-and-go is a version of setting up the next ruck where instead of the scrum half or acting scrum half passing the ball to charge forwards, the forward picks the ball up directly off the ground and charges forwards. They might then encounter only one opposition player before going to ground. The next

The ball is on the ground. This is a ruck.

Where is the ball? On the ground, it's a ruck; in hand, it's a maul. Players lying on the ground are not allowed to compete.

teammate immediately picks up the ball and charges forwards again. This is repeated again and again.

Ending a ruck

A ruck ends when the ball comes out (is beyond the hindmost feet) or is on or over the goal line. If the ruck stops moving, the ref allows time for it to start again before blowing his whistle. In that case, or if the ball becomes unplayable, the referee awards a scrum to the team that was moving forwards. If neither team was moving forwards, then the scrum is awarded to the team that was moving forwards before the ruck formed. If neither team was, a scrum is set and the put-in goes to the attacking team.

> ### Drills
> - *Forming a ruck; binding and driving.*
> - *Enter from the rear — set up a ruck, place cones as "the gate" and have the players enter between them.*
> - *Practise the various offside options at a ruck.*
> - *Digging out a stuck ball.*
> - *Set up ruck scenarios, with some players not in it, then have them to decide whether to enter it or not.*
> - *Pick-and-go.*
> - *Pick-and-go race between two sets of forwards.*
> - *Opposed rucking on a gradient up to match intensity (wearing padding) including over players that have gone to ground so the players in the ruck do not trip over (use tackle bags for the fallen players).*

MAUL

Maul defined

This is the definition of a maul from the laws: A maul begins when a player carrying the ball is held by one or more opponents, and one or more of the ball-carrier's teammates bind on the ball carrier. A maul therefore consists, when it begins, of at least three players, all on their feet; the ball carrier and one player from each team. All the players involved must be caught in or bound to the maul and must be on their feet and moving towards a goal line.

Forming or joining a maul

The rules are the same as for a ruck: on the feet, from behind the hindmost feet, proper binding, heads and shoulders no lower than the hips. As new teammates arrive at the maul, they are effectively forming a wedge either side of the ball carrier, shielding the ball from the opposition. Also, a player must not try to drag an opponent out of a maul.

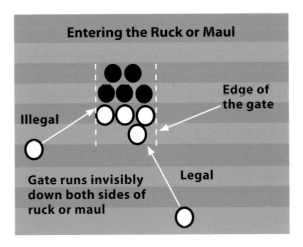

Offside at the maul

Same as for a ruck, although if players detach from a maul so that there are no players of the defending team left in it, their offside line runs through the foremost opposition foot in the maul. Defending players can rejoin this maul by the first player binding on the first opposition player in the maul.

Stripping the ball

Often the ball can be "stolen" when a maul is part-formed with an opposition player still wrestling for the ball. When trying to wrestle the ball from another player, it is more effective to use the force of the whole body, through the shoulder, wrenching through the ball, rather than just using the arm.

The driving maul

The purpose of the maul is to secure possession, but if the maul is going forwards, the attacking side — usually instructed by their scrum half — might decide to continue driving forwards to gain ground. The ball should be carried by a player in the second row or at the back of the maul to protect it from the opposition. In this kind of maul, the leading forwards may be fairly upright, but those behind should adopt a low body position to push the maul forwards. The drive should be continued for as long as the maul is moving forwards. Once the maul becomes stationary a change of tactics must be employed: either the ball is released to the backs or it is moved to other players in a position to continue progress with a rolling maul.

The rolling maul

The rolling maul is similar to the driving maul, except that when the maul becomes stationary the attacking team smuggles the ball to the side of the maul where the defence seems weakest (the ball must always travel backwards, of course). The player with the ball then rolls out to the side, tightly supported by teammates. The other forwards peel off the original maul and support the new movement. As the defending team regroups and "plugs the gap", the ball is again smuggled to another part of the maul to change the point of attack. A rolling maul could theoretically continue indefinitely in this way. It should be coordinated by the scrum half, who is in the best position to see what is happening. A rolling maul is often a good tactic for scoring a try from a line out near the opponent's line.

Truck & trailer

If the attacking team's part of a maul is made up of (or breaks into) two distinct sections with the ball in the rear one, the referee might consider that the front group are obstructing the opposition and will

On the feet — ball in hand; this is a maul.

The Italian team practises a rolling maul at training.

award a penalty. This has been given the descriptive name of "truck and trailer".

Ending a maul

A maul ends when the ball or a player with the ball leaves the maul, when the ball is on the ground (in which case it becomes a ruck), or when the maul is over the goal line.

Referee ends maul

If the ball carrier in a maul goes to ground, the maul collapses (not as a result of foul play), remains stationary or has stopped moving forwards for longer than five seconds, the referee ends it and awards a scrum to the team not in possession when the maul began ("use it or lose it"). If the ref is not sure who had possession, the scrum is awarded to the team moving forwards before the maul stopped. If the maul was completely stationary, the attacking team gets the scrum.

Maul after kick

If a player catches the ball directly from an opponent's kick (except from a kickoff or a dropout), the player is immediately held by an opponent and a maul forms and becomes stationary for longer than five seconds, or if the ball becomes unplayable, then the put-in at the scrum goes to the catcher's team.

Ruck & maul infringements

Mauls cannot be pre-formed. Two illegal types of mauls are "flying wedge" (players binding together and charging from a distance) and the "cavalry charge" (players charging forwards in a line).

When a maul becomes a ruck

If a maul collapses (not intentionally) and the ball goes to ground then that is now a ruck. However,

Drills
- *Forming a maul.*
- *Stripping the ball.*
- *Binding and driving.*
- *Enter from the rear — set up a maul, place cones and have the players enter between them.*
- *Practise the various offside options at a maul.*
- *Channelling back the ball through the maul.*
- *Rejoining the maul.*
- *Driving maul.*
- *Rolling maul.*
- *A maul that becomes a ruck.*
- *Mauling against tackle bags.*
- *Contested mauling.*
- *Mauling over fallen players (use tackle bags) so that players in the maul do not trip over them.*
- *Ask each player what is the difference between a ruck and maul.*
- *Set up various scenarios and get them to say if it is a ruck or a maul.*
- *Set up various ruck or maul situations; before they enter each, they must shout whether it is a ruck or a maul and execute the correct technique. In the end they must get this 100 per cent right. Then they know it.*

a ruck never develops into a maul for the simple reason that when a ball is in a ruck, it is illegal to pick it up off the ground (and a maul has the ball in the hand). Some open play must occur before a new maul could form after a ruck.

Ruck and maul motto:
Rucks and mauls move forwards.

12 DEFENCE

Defence more than anything is a state of mind. It is harder and more demanding than attack. In a tight match against very good opposition it sometimes feels like a player is making tackle after tackle after tackle. Only when they are prepared to tackle for the whole game will the tide turn. Defence is like a wild animal hunting its prey. It takes concentration, careful application, persistence and patience.

IT ALL STARTS WITH DEFENCE

Good defence provides the opportunity for attack. It is the springboard. Players also talk about "earning the right to play". That means if they do all the hard, sometimes boring or difficult little things well — running, taking up position, marking, supporting, tackling — that is what will eventually put them into the position to do the really exciting things well, like breaking through the opposition defensive line and running full speed, ball in hand, towards their line.

Defence motto: tackling is an individual responsibility: defence is a team responsibility.

THE PILLARS OF DEFENCE

1. Position — every player should know their defensive position in every situation. It is up to the coach to devise this and communicate it to players.

The Rebels' line has been breached and they are outnumbered. Now they must scramble back in cover.

For example, at set play, the wingers and fullback should be back to accept a kick. But the wingers should also be ready to move up into the line if the opposition runs the ball.

2. Marking — in a defensive line, every player in the team is responsible for marking a member of the opposing team (usually the one who is standing opposite them). That means covering that player and staying with them, almost like a mirror image, then quickly closing them down when they are about to receive the ball.

3. Aggression — limit the opposition's space. Hit hard in the tackle.

4. Tackling — when an opposition player gets the ball, the defender marking that player must make an effective tackle. Virtually all scores track back to a missed tackle.

5. Communication — situations can change rapidly in rugby. An attacking side can change its angles, run decoys and use all sorts of deceptive ploys to try and trick the opposition. The defence counters this by shouting to each other to let players know who is marking whom and which defensive patterns they are using.

6. Concentration — defence takes concentration and hard work. You are under siege. The Vikings invaders are charging at you and you have to resist them. Only on defence do you really get to touch that resilience of spirit that goes deep to the roots of a person's being.

7. Discipline — defence takes discipline (purpose and persistence). No matter how much talent a person

Well-organized defence by the All Blacks. Players in a line, evenly spaced and marking up their opposition.

Good crowding defence by the All Blacks. Wallaby Drew Mitchell has nowhere to go.

has, it will be wasted unless they use discipline to guide and control it. The two act together to create success. Defence is almost all discipline. You have to momentarily bury your talent. But the discipline of defence is what gives the opportunity for your talent to flourish again, when you are able to turn defence into attack.

Defensive systems

Teams evolve systems (pre-set plans) for how they are going to deal with opposition attacks. There are three basic types in modern rugby: player-on-player, drift defence, and rush defence. Variations of these can be used in specific situations, such as defending a move off the back of the scrum near a team's own goal line. It is crucial that every player on the team is aware of the pattern used, and sticks to it in the pressure of a match situation.

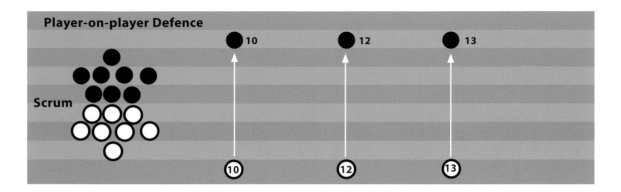

Player-on-player defence

In player-on-player defence, the players of a defending team tackle the player directly opposite them, as shown in the diagram above. But if the fullback enters the line, then the inside player nearest them takes them. There is also a variation of player-on-player defence in which the open-side flanker takes the fly half, especially when their own fly half is not a good tackler. After that each player takes their own opponent.

Drift defence

In drift defence (diagram below), the open-side flanker (white 7 in the diagram below) comes off the scrum or the back of the line out to challenge the opposing fly half (black 10). The defending team's fly half (white 10) then takes the opposition's inside centre (black 12) and so on. Therefore, the defending team's players are not taking the player opposite them but the next one out and they have to "drift" across the field to make the tackle.

This drifting angle pushes the attacking team sideways across the field towards the touchline, giving them less space to work in. It also allows for an extra player in the defensive team to take the fullback if they enter the line. This extra player would normally be the outside centre, but if the fullback comes into the line in another position, one of the other players would have to tackle them. Also, the angle of the drift follows the ball, so if the ball carrier passes, then the tackler is running in the right direction to make the tackle.

This type of defence is also known as player-out defence or one-out defence, because the tackler is tackling the player outside them.

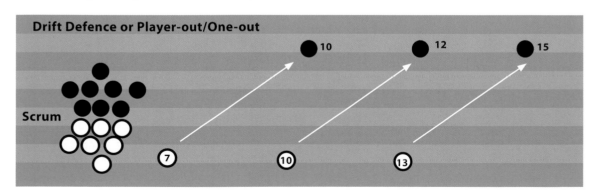

Outside-in defence

A variation of this is the outside-in defence, in which the defensive pattern starts marking players from the wing inward, towards the scrum. In this variation, tacklers are lining up on the outside shoulder of their opponent, coming at them on an angle.

Rush defence

Rush defence is a form of outside-in defence in which the defenders rush up rapidly on the attackers. Because they are aiming towards the outside shoulder and the ball is coming from the inside, the attackers are looking the wrong way, which puts them under more pressure.

Blind-side defence

The keys to stopping an attack (from the white number eight in the diagram opposite) that comes down the narrower channel of the blind side of the field are compressing the space and an early tackle. This is the responsibility first of the blind-side flanker (black 7), supported by the scrum half (black 9) and the number eight. Scrum halves should be communicating with the back row as soon as they get any indication the opposition is preparing to make a blind-side attack.

Defending wingers on the blind side usually hang back, marking the opposing winger, but if the other defenders are slow, or if they read the move

The defensive line (left) is diagonal and will drift outwards, trying to push the opposition attack over the touchline.

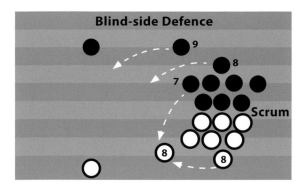

Blind-side Defence

9

8

7

Scrum

8

8

each knowing what is expected of them in that particular scenario. Due to the time pressure, any communications between them will be short and barked. If necessary they should work out a shorthand code — for example, "R2" meaning "move two paces to your right". Or they might call the code name for a defensive pattern. The backs are more used to this, and at such times they should direct the forwards in the defensive line.

early, they can rush in and make the tackle, but they have to make sure the tackle will be successful before they start their run, or they will leave a huge gap behind them.

Unit defence

A team's defensive systems are set before a match, but break down as situations change and also as players tire. In open play, whatever players are nearest the ball must form units of defence. What each does in the situation should be largely instinctive, based on them training together;

Offensive defence

Offensive defence is a strategy and series of strong tackles to drive the opposition backwards even though they are the attackers.

PRACTISING DEFENCE

At training, teams often instinctively practise general play and moves going forwards. They should also practise defence going backwards. Players should know where they are supposed to be and what they are supposed to do in all defensive situations. They should be challenged and pressured just as they would be in a real match.

Pressure defence from the Wallabies means South Africa are struggling to retain the ball.

Drills
- *Player-on-player defence.*
- *Drift defence.*
- *Outside-in defence.*
- *Rush defence.*
- *Blind-side defence.*
- *Unit defence.*
- *Offensive defence.*
- *Defending the try line.*
- *Whole team desperate defence going backwards.*
- *Defence against all the attacking moves outlined in the following chapter on attack.*

13 ATTACK

Attack is the fun part of rugby. There is nothing more thrilling than watching a long period of continuous attack and counter-attack between two teams.

THE THEORY OF ATTACK

A rugby field is a rectangle of limited space cluttered up by 30 players and one referee. There is only so much space so, in attack, you have to create it.

Space is the key

A prolific goal-scorer in football (soccer) once said, "If I find the space in the penalty area [the rectangle in front of the goal] the ball comes to me". In rugby, when you find the space, you score the try. If you look at a list of the leading international try-scorers, you will find they are all wingers. On a rugby field most of the space is on the outside.

Scoring on the inside

A defensive line is like an elastic band. The attacker tries to pull it in to create space on the outside. When they score on the inside, either the band has been stretched wide or they have created a small pocket of space by piercing through it. Or they kick over the defensive line and use the space behind it.

You can go through, over or around a defensive line. Through is the tanks (force) or the spies (deception), over is the air force (kicking) and around is the cavalry (wings).

Space, no space

Attacks should be launched towards open space; if that space becomes defended, the ball is shifted, sooner or later, to where the next space opens up. Over a long period of possession and attack, spaces will open up.

Plan of attack

Attacking plans should be based on the strengths of the players in the team, such as a strong centre or a fast winger. The attacking team should have several moves they can use in a match: they should have moves that form the units of sequences of attacks but, of course, in attack there is much that will be created spontaneously.

Above: *The next rule of attack is to try and evade defenders.*
Left: *Justin Mensah-Coker of Canada applies the first rule of attack — go forward with the ball.*

PARTS OF AN ATTACK

There are six basic parts to an attacking move: the roles played by the providers, the playmaker, the penetrator, the supporters, the deliverer, and the finisher.

1. **Providers:** The providers are the players who do the build-up work, wearing away the opposition defence and committing them to tackles, or rucks and mauls. They set up the platform, by putting the opposition defence under pressure, and this causes holes and opportunities to appear.

2. **Playmaker:** The playmaker is the player who creates the time or space to launch the attack. Their job is to get behind the opposition's defensive line, either themselves or to put someone through it or to kick over it.

3. **Penetrator:** The penetrator is the player who breaks through, or penetrates, the opposition's defensive line. They might be the strong and tricky centre who breaks the lines, but they are seldom the finisher, because the cover defence will usually come across and cut them off.

4. **Supporters:** The supporters are the players who back up the penetrator. As soon as the line is broken there should be a whole flood of them at pace to take advantage of the opportunity.

5. **Deliverer:** The deliverer provides the final pass or kick before the try is scored. This is a great skill because it requires timing, patience and killer instinct.

6. **Finisher:** The finisher is the one who scores.

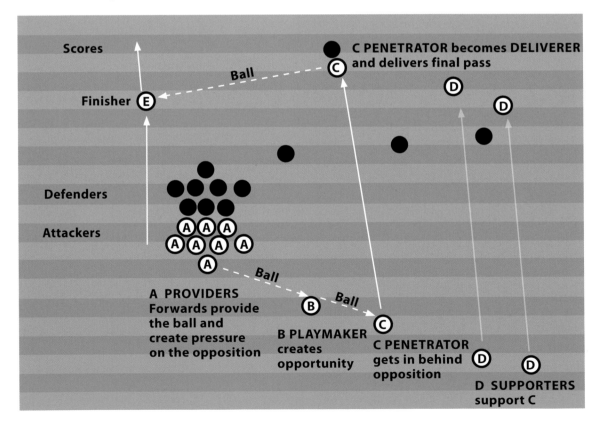

Theory of the parts of an attack

These roles are just temporary labels to highlight particular skills. In a solo try where the player strips the ball in the tackle and runs the length of the field to score, the try-scorer would be provider, playmaker, penetrator and finisher all in one. So don't get too serious about these names or you will lose the pure joy of creativity that is the essence of an attack. Any player can take on any of these roles. A number eight might penetrate the line with a surging run; a prop might be the playmaker and kick the ball through for the winger to run on to. And, of course, anybody can score a try.

Communication on attack

Communication is as important on attack as it is on defence. Players call moves, such as to come in for a pass, run forwards during kicks and so on. When in support, they call out to ball carriers to let them know they are there.

Quality ball

The first key is the forwards providing the backs with quality ball (also known as front-foot ball). Quality ball comes back quickly, cleanly and accurately, before the opposition can regroup. When the forwards are not really making a dent in the defence, then the attacking side can get impatient and frustrated. They start going lateral, "push the pass", and that is when interceptions occur (one team catching the ball thrown by the other team). Planned moves should be canceled if the ball comes back slow or with the opposition defence set so there is little chance of success. Then it is up to the forwards to set up better-quality ball. When the quality of the ball is so bad that it puts the attacking team under pressure, or their forwards are being driven back, then the only option is to kick.

Ma'a Nonu seeks to penetrate the Australian defensive line.

BASIC ATTACKING MOVES

Miss-out or cut-out pass

Bypasses a player in the attacking line, spreading the ball wide more quickly.

Scissors pass

Ball carrier cuts across in front of one of their own players and then twists to pass it back to their teammate (the lines of the two players cross each other like the blades of an open pair of scissors). The player who ends up with the ball can effectively change the angle of attack.

Loop

The ball carrier passes the ball then runs around behind the receiver to take another pass, effectively creating themself as an extra player.

Pickup from the scrum

The number eight picks up the ball from the scrum and breaks towards the blind or open side, supported by the scrum half and the nearest flanker.

Blind-side attack

Players move from the open side to the blind side, seeking to outnumber the defenders there.

Scrum-half dart

There are channels close to a set play or a ruck or maul that are often little blind spots in defence, which the scrum half can dart through.

Kicking behind the line

Chip kicks, grubbers, cross kicks, high kicks etc. Before kicking, either make the defenders stop or try to pull them forwards to commit them and so deceive them.

Ryan Nicholas of Japan spots a gap. But will it close before he can breach the defence?

Decoy runners

Many pre-planned moves use decoy runners to draw defenders out of position.

Player running from depth

This is especially effective when the playmaker has caused the defenders to stand still and the new attacker comes through at pace.

Fullback into the line

This creates an extra player, change of angle and they can enter at any point, but should always enter at the latest possible moment to create the biggest surprise.

Wing coming into the line

The best place for a winger to come off their wing is often close in to a scrum, ruck or maul, where play is static, or appearing suddenly on their opposite wing to create an overlap.

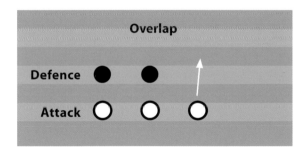

Changing the angle of attack

This throws out the natural flatness of a defence. Attack the opposition in 3D!

Cut-back pass

A typical example is the outside centre drifting towards the outside, cramping up the field. The correct action in this case is for the wing to cut in behind them and the centre passes back to them with a cut-back pass (similar to the scissors move).

Double-switch

The attacking team moves the ball wide (to the left, for example). As the defence moves to cover them, they switch the ball to the right. As the defence converges here, the ball is immediately switched back left again.

ATTACKING SEQUENCES

Moves from set play

These are easier to plan, because you know where the opposition will be on the field. They are harder to execute because they know roughly where you are. The trick is to devise a move that must pull one or more opposition players out of position in a way that you can outnumber them. This might involve, for example, setting up a false ruck that they are drawn into or decoy runners that pull defenders across to the wrong side of the scrum.

Middle attack

The value of an attack in the middle of the field, usually either through the forwards or the centres, is that, if stopped, it gives the attacking team the option of going left or right.

Layers of defence

One move alone will not usually cut open a defence. Once the penetrator has got through the first line of defence, the second defensive line — the fullback and the covering wings — will start to converge on them. One way to practise this at training is to have five against three + three. Five attackers have to get past a line of three defenders, then they have to get past the next line of three defenders. There are an infinite number of scenarios of this type which can be devised and practised to get through multiple layers of defence.

Keeping an attack going

Attacks can move forwards in close play by a mix of the forwards driving up and short-passing to a teammate in support.

Touchline to touchline

This involves stretching the opposition across to one side of the field, then bringing it back across the other side where gaps might now be appearing. But you can't just go side to side or the opposition would smash you. In between there will be several rucks and mauls to draw in the defenders.

Penalty after desperate defence

Defenders are often crowded at the point of penalty and moving the ball wide quickly or with a cross kick often finds the defence thin or non-existent out wide.

Counter-attack

A counter-attack is an attack by the team that was previously on defence. They get a turnover and are suddenly in possession. This is a great time to attack, because the opposition has no defensive structure.

Counter-attack in opposition territory

Depending on the situation, often the best route is straight ahead, before they have any time to recover, even if their players are nearby. They will be scrambling back, magnetized and cramped into the point of attack, while the team now attacking is coming forwards and should also be spreading out.

Counter-attack from own territory

In this case, it is usually better to move the ball wide quickly away from the contact area and run forwards at pace towards where the big spaces are. Then it is a wild cavalry charge up the field, with new attackers racing to support the ball carrier. The trick is to keep up the pace before the defence can recover.

Returning the ball from deep

After fielding a high kick, the key factor for the fullback is how much time they have before the opposition chase arrives. The closer the chasers, the more they usually play safe. If the chasers are slow, the returner should run towards them at three-quarters pace, considering their options. Even if they decide to run, their body language should always imply they're going to kick to keep the opposition guessing (unless there is a wide gap in front of them and they decide to go for it straight away). Often they should not decide what they are going to do until the last minute, which is when the chasers are almost in tackling range. The options are usually to kick (no support), run (if there is space or fast support nearby), or to set up a ruck (if there is close or slow support nearby).

All Black fullback Israel Dagg counter-attacks to score.

The back three

The wingers and the fullback form a fast and very exciting attacking unit. They should have a good understanding with many strategies worked out in advance, so that when one of them takes the ball, the others are already taking an angle to support them.

Setting up a drop goal

The best location to kick from is just outside the opposing 22, in the middle of the field. To get that prime position, the attacking team might need to set up a ruck or maul about 10 metres in advance. This allows time to pass the ball and for the kicker to set themselves and execute the kick, before chasing defenders can charge it down.

Setting up a drop goal from deep

In a match where time is running out and a drop goal will win it, if the attacking team is too far away, they need to engineer a move, or moves, that gets them close enough, so that sooner or later they will be in a position to win a penalty or take a drop kick at goal.

Drills
- *All of the moves in this chapter with variations in units of two to three players.*
- *Various overlap scenarios.*
- *Two players against one in a grid.*
- *Three players against two.*
- *All of the moves in this chapter with variations, the entire back line involved unopposed in units.*
- *The back three working as a unit.*
- *The entire back line against no one, then against three up to seven players (the defenders only have to touch the ball, or the player in possession of it, with two hands on the player).*
- *Multiple layers of defence.*
- *Counter-attack from various positions and scenarios.*
- *Beating the last line of defence.*
- *Timing the final pass.*
- *Scoring.*

The trick to a drop goal is in creating the time and space beforehand.

14 OPTIONS

It is the Rugby World Cup final. Time is up on the clock. Your team is winning by one point. You hold the ball in your hands. You are five metres from the touchline. What are you going to do? Yes, you only have one option, the simple option — kick the ball out!

The first rule of option-taking — always take the simple option.

RISK & REWARD

Option just means choice. The choice you are making can be between success and disaster. What is the risk of the action? What is the reward of the action? You take the option which provides the most reward and the least risk.

The scale of risk

This is measured by the field. If the field is 100 metres long, then the most risk is on your own goal line and the most reward is on the opponent's goal line. On the halfway line, the risk and reward is 50/50 (50 metres each way).

The risk increases

Now you lose the ball 30 metres from your own goal line. The risk increases. Now it is 70/30 against you. That means you have to run 70 metres to score, but your opponent only has to run 30. What about when it gets down to 95/5. Big risk. The opponent is camped right on your goal line.

Risk/reward ratio

Ratio is a rate of comparison. So the risk/reward ratio compares risk against reward. In every situation, in life, as well as rugby, you have to compare the risk against the reward. If something contains so much risk that it puts your entire reward in jeopardy, don't do it.

Rugby risk/reward ratio

In rugby, the risk/reward ratio has to do with three factors.

1. How close you are to your own try line.
2. The score of the game.
3. How likely it is that the option chosen will succeed.

The score

If one team is ahead, they should generally take fewer risks to protect their lead. However, the team that is behind might have to take more risks in order to catch up.

A situation

In a Super 15 rugby semi-final match, one team was just behind on the scoreboard. In their own 22, with plenty of time left on the clock, they tried to do a chip over the heads of the opposition line to run the length of the field and score. But the opposition managed to get the ball and score.

Left: Victory depends on taking the right options.

Celebration after a try — but players must get their "game face" on again before the restart.

A poor option

This was a very poor option. To run the length of the field from their own 22 was a bit of a long shot. That they would regain possession from a chip was also uncertain. To do it so close to the line was way too big a risk. And so it proved. They did not need to take big risks because there was plenty of time left and they were only one score behind. But with the opposition scoring, they only put more pressure on themselves. Now they were two scores behind. On the scale of risk, they should have been at least another 30 or 40 metres up the field before even considering the option they chose.

Options after scoring

Most teams get too relaxed immediately after scoring and often give away a try. The opposition will be looking to hit back, so the team that just scored should tighten everything up and offer them no opportunities.

A CLOSE MATCH

In a close match, neither team can afford to take risks. In test match rugby, the winning team is usually the one that makes the least mistakes. That also means taking the least risks. That is not to say a team should play defensively. It just means calculating each risk based on the risk/reward ratio and the scale of risk.

BEST OPTIONS

The best option to take will vary with the circumstances of the situation and the position:

Defending on own line — situation one

Situation: A team is under great pressure on its own line and gets the ball.

Best option: Kick it to touch.

Defending on own line — situation two

Situation: A team is under great pressure on their own line and get the ball. Time is up on the clock, and they are behind by three points.

Best option: Run the ball and try to keep it alive. The only chance of winning the game is to score at the other end of the field.

Attacking two on one — situation one

Situation: The ball carrier is facing the opposition fullback. Outside, the wing is unmarked.

Best option: The ball carrier draws the fullback and passes to the wing.

Attacking two on one — situation two

Situation: The ball carrier is facing the opposition fullback. Outside, the wing is also marked, but the attacking fullback is coming up fast in support.

Possible option: Kick behind the opposing wing so the attacking fullback can run on to the ball.

A situation develops. Which options the attackers and defenders take will decide if a try is scored or not.

15 COACHING

A coach is a leader, teacher and guide and sets the standard. The coach should continually challenge the players and seek to improve them, both as players and as people. This will result in better performance of the team as a whole.

TEAM SELECTION

The first rule of team selection is "select either the player for the plan or the plan for the player". When putting a team together, decide what ingredients you require and set down the requirements for each position. Write these down and keep going back to them as you search for and select your players. Exhaust every avenue until you find the players that most closely match your requirements.

Seek outstanding players

Not necessarily stars, but players who will be reliable in the position they hold and will not be found wanting when the heat is on. These would be distributed throughout the team, ideally in the front row (the point of contact with the opposition), one of the halves (as playmaker) and fullback (last line of defence). Other key positions are open-side flanker, number eight (linking forwards and backs and taking the ball forwards from the back of the scrum) and the centres (the collision point in the backs). Get good players in these positions and you can build a team around them.

GOALS

Once the players are identified and notified, they must be part of a long-term goal. The management team, captain, vice-captains, players' committee, senior players and all members of the squad should all know and agree with the team's long-term goal. There must be no hidden agendas.

The long-term goal is achieved by setting and meeting short-term goals. Short-term goals must be realistic. Even smaller goals can then be set, which might be performance-related rather than scoreboard-related. Keep things basic and keep things simple. Improved performance leads to improved results. The most effective plan evolves slowly so that there is a continuous but gradual improvement throughout the team.

YOU AS COACH

- Be honest, both to yourself and your players. Never lie to them and if you need to criticize them, tell it straight.
- You are the coach, the guide and the manager, but your most important role is not as a talker but as a listener, because you are also the problem solver.
- Don't try to do it all yourself. Share the problem and use the abilities of the team to help solve it.
- Don't be too proud. If you don't know how to solve a problem a player is experiencing, find someone who can.

Like most top coaches, Robbie Deans has a lot on his mind, and his hands full.

A good coach pays attention to every detail and makes sure it is right.

The players

- Raise your players' self-esteem and always strive to maintain it.
- Stimulate the players and encourage them to think about and discover their own solutions to problems. Encourage an open mind.
- Ensure each player knows their role. Test them on it. Don't let them get confused.
- Be realistic. It is unreasonable to expect excellence right away. Don't undermine your players' confidence by expecting them to be of a high standard too soon.
- Get them to seek improved performance ahead of seeking results on the scoreboard.

A strong team ethic

Team responsibility means that each player is responsible for every other player. It is the old three musketeers' chant of "all for one and one for all". There should be no blame in a match. If one player drops a ball or misses a tackle in a match, then every player in that team works harder to make up for it, and at training the players help each other practise the cause of the mistake until it becomes a strong skill. Sometimes people's greatest strengths come from what was once a weakness. Each team member supports and encourages the others to grow as players and as people.

Training

- Practices should be planned. Write down the tasks on cards and keep the cards for later reference. Be organized and stick tightly to times and schedules.

- Structure the practice so it involves the whole squad. Work on communication and teamwork. Aim for mistake-free activity. Make it enjoyable.
- Tell the players what you want to achieve at the beginning of each training session.
- Share the "voice load" at practice. Get the players to take responsibility for some of it.
- Encourage players to communicate constructively about the tasks at hand but be firm about idle or destructive chatter.
- Do the accuracy drills early in training, as the fatigue players experience later in the session will reduce their thinking and skill levels.

TEAM PATTERN

The first thing the coach and the team have to do is decide on the pattern of rugby they wish to play. They have to answer five basic questions:

1. How are we going to win possession of the ball?
2. How are we going to retain possession of the ball?
3. How are we going to use the ball?
4. What defensive patterns will the opposition use?
5. How committed will the defence be?

Involvement

Coaches have to make sure the whole team is involved. They should want every player to contribute 100 per cent. They must also plan strategies and tactics that take advantage of the actual strengths of the team. One player may have exceptional speed. Another may be able to kick long clearing distances with their left foot. The coach must take advantage of these talents in the attacking and defensive plans. When you join the energy resources of the players to a realistic plan, success will come.

> **Drill**
> As a team, practise match scenarios where everything goes wrong, then the team rises to the challenge and overcomes them.

Patterns and moves have to be practised over and over again in training until perfect.

16 TACTICS

The great Chinese general Sun Tzu tells the story of a small army in retreat from a larger one. The general of the larger army was known to be very proud.

So when the smaller army arrived at a large rock, it painted a message about him on it. Then the smaller army deliberately held off the larger army until darkness was almost falling. When the larger army's forward troops saw the rock, they sent news of it back to their general. He hurried forwards to see it for himself. By now it was dark, so he was surrounded by torchbearers. As the torches arrived at the rock, waiting in the distance, all the archers of the smaller army fired their arrows at the light. The general was killed.

The battle was won. The smaller army beat the larger army by tactics.

TACTICS DEFINED

Tactics means using the strengths of your team, the weaknesses of the opposition (even their strengths if you are really clever), and the circumstances of the situation, all to your advantage, in order to win.

Your most powerful weapon

Rugby is a game of strength, speed, skill and will. The last of these — will — will always be superior to brute strength, lightning speed and silky skills because your mind is the best weapon you possess.

Above: *The attackers seek to outmanoeuvre the opposition and put a teammate into undefended space to score.*
Left: *The first tactic in rugby is strength.*

THE KEY TO TACTICS

Know your own team well and know your opposition better than they know themselves.

A winning team

Rugby is a game played by a group of 15 individuals on the field at any one time.

• With practise they become a team.
• With communication they become one mind.
• With fitness, they become one body.
• With tactics they share one goal.
• With perseverance they succeed.

BASIC TACTICS

There are several basic types of tactics that a coach might select before a game, or the players might select and change during a game as the situation demands.

Watertight defence

Play safe. Play territory. Do the simple things well. Eliminate mistakes. A skilled boxer does not try and knock the opponent out with the first punch. First they keep some distance and feel them out. Get their length and their timing. They take as few blows as possible and try to get a sense of how this particular opponent can be beaten.

Force — straight down the middle

The two sets of forwards meet like pounding waves of the sea. Which one is stronger? Your forwards might be bigger, stronger, tougher or more aggressive, smashing through the weaker defences of the opposition. Who wins the collision is always the first question asked in a game. This is the next safest tactic to adopt and if the opposition is weak, this is where you score the first-round knockout.

Pressure

If they resist, then the battle to see who is stronger takes longer and this takes pressure. Then it becomes a war of attrition. You apply a continuous pressure to wear them down and force cracks in their defence and their resolve, to provide opportunities for your team.

Pace

This is the killer blow, the lightning raid, the moment that can turn a game if you have players of genuine pace. If the opposition are poor defenders against this weapon, you use it again and again to shred their defence and their spirit.

Outstanding player(s)

You have players who are superior in strength, speed, skill or cleverness. Frame your game plan to take advantage of their skills in a way that will

Utilize your stars, such as electric winger Hosea Gear.

Use sustained pressure to create gaps in the defensive line.

benefit your team. That might be feeding them the ball often. But it also might require that you do proper preparatory work first, such as wearing down the defence or lulling it into a sense of false security.

Skill

When teams are evenly matched, skill becomes the key factor, from the little skills done well, to strategic kicking that torments the opposition, to individual brilliance or the well-executed team move that opens up the opposition defence.

Tactical cunning

What is the exact formula that will open up the opposition? It might only be one factor, well planned, executed with care and repeated often, working at the opposition like a piece of strong steel that if bent back and forth enough times will eventually crack.

Fitness

Tight matches are usually won in the last 10 minutes. By then tiredness is starting to set in and so courage, resolve and skill levels reduce. Be fitter than the opposition and outlast them.

THE WILL TO WIN

Make your team ready to play and hungry to win. Empower their spirits and devise tactics that will break the spirit of the other team. One team has to decide to give up. When neither team makes that decision, that is when the great matches are played.

Decision

Sometimes it feels that a match is decided by decision alone beforehand. That was what happened in the 1995 Rugby World Cup final when South Africa beat a superior All Black side because the whole South African nation needed the victory to reunify their country. Just as in 2011, the All Blacks defended a one point lead for 30 minutes with simply the will to win.

WINNING TACTICS

Rugby has been described as chess with muscles. Most matches between chess grandmasters end in a draw. A rugby team should go into every match prepared to win it just 3–0. They start with a firm defensive base and build from there, always hungry to create time, space and the opportunity to break out into sudden offense.

The goal on attack is to cut loose, run wild and free; and score. The goal on defence is to smother, stifle and frustrate the opposition: don't give them the ball, any time, or any opportunity to do anything with it; allow them only the scraps; and stop them scoring. With tactics a team tries to outmanoeuvre or outlast the opposition.

Attitude

Attitude has to be right or a game can be lost before it starts. Many teams are in awe of the All Blacks before they even take the field. In recent years the Welsh team has tried to counter this by referring to them in training only as "New Zealand".

Once there was a schoolboy team that was short of players. When the teams shook hands before the game, older, physically intimidating players of that school joined the line-up. They didn't actually play in the game, but the other team was so spooked that they played against their shadows and lost the match.

Be patient, stay alert and win the little battles. An older team playing a younger one knows they have to frustrate youthful exuberance until it explodes back on itself. You can also tire out a bigger team with superior fitness, and tactics that make them run around like hamsters in a cage. And put effort

Leaders will arise. Cometh the hour; cometh the man.

Kick cleverly to move forward up the field.

Do the simple things to retain possession.

In tight games, kick every available penalty goal.

even into the small things, such as players trying to make an extra yard after each tackle.

The four Ps — possession, position, pressure & points

A match begins — two teams, 15 players each, all fit and fresh. The first tactic is to try and go right through the middle of the opposition. They hold firm. So now you play a phase game, trying to keep possession of the ball for as long as possible, trying to get over the gain line, drawing them into your plan for the game, making them work and follow.

You apply the four Ps. The first priority is possession, the second is position (territory), the third is pressure, the fourth is points. Apply continuous pressure to disrupt their structures, drawing their defenders into the breakdown, always seeking to isolate and outnumber them on a part of the field, or a part of the game, such as a ruck.

Minimize the opposition's opportunities to

have the ball or do anything with it. If they have possession, put pressure on them, hunt for turnovers, and make them fall short of what they are trying to do.

Going forwards — momentum

The overriding necessity in any game is to keep going forwards. Sometimes some forwards seem to barely handle the ball during an entire match, but they are working hard to get the momentum of the team going forwards. Refer to Isaac Newton's theories on inertia and momentum. Inertia is the tendency of a mass to remain unmoving unless moved. But if a mass is moving it has momentum and so has the potential to get even faster. Commentators talk about the "change of momentum" in a game.

This change of momentum does not come about by accident, but by a lot of players doing a lot of little things right or one player doing one big thing

Then when the break comes, here by Sonny Bill Williams, flood through the gap in full support.

right. You need a long lever to move a huge rock but first you might need to use small levers to get the large one in position. Everyone in the team needs to understand how and when to apply the right set of levers to the actual situation they are faced with. Sometimes the lever is as small as a slight change of body position going into the tackle, or you wield the big lever and the tough forward smashes through several tackles or the pacey back flies down the wing.

Countering the opposition

The other necessity is to get the opposition going backwards or at least to stop them from going forwards, as well as trying to make them lose their shape, their pattern and their systems.

Keep prodding and probing for weaknesses. If a team or player is suspected of having a weakness under the high ball, test them. If there is a weak tackler in their backs, target them. If their defence rushes up flat, chip over it. If they have a weakness at the scrum, expose it.

If they are weak in the line out, kick to touch more. Wherever they are vulnerable — attack it.

Maintain the pressure and continue to create opportunities, ever alert for holes and space for your own forces to spill through or into. Your fly half should always be reading the play and deciding the next tactic. If the match is close, moves should be kept tight and low-risk such as picking up from the back of the scrum, attacking straight from a maul or line out, blind side from the scrum, high kicks, long kicks etc. Sometimes teams engage in "ping-pong" with the fullbacks and other players standing deep, kicking the ball high to each other, waiting for the other to make a mistake. Play this game if *you* want to; not if *they* want to.

Dictating the tactics

The sequence of tactics used in a game is tight play, midfield play and wide play. Going wide too early against good opposition is asking for trouble, so first take the ball up in the midfield. Try to outmanoeuvre and deceive the opposition, shifting the ball around, changing the focus of attack, looking for the opening. Increase the pace and see if the opposition can keep up. Force them to take risks, while you keep your defence firm, and reset your defence immediately after each passage of play.

Both teams are wrestling to control the game, to dictate its direction, tempo and territory, but don't lose sight of the need to keep the scoreboard ticking over — take any penalties within kicking range, kick any drop goals within range if their defence is strong and your attack is making no progress. Your playmakers and the whole team should always be alert for any opportunity to counter-attack. Many of the tries scored in international matches are by counter-attack as defences are normally very strong.

Keeping it moving

As the match opens up, judge which moves to use and when: there is no point calling a move unless there is a good chance it will come off. Some moves may work better later in the match when the opposition defence tires. Start moving the ball out wider from the contact area, then, as a breakthrough suddenly arises, flood support players into the gap.

Players should support on both sides of the ball carrier. Keep up the pace and continuity of the attack, and as it nears the try line, concentrate hard and be ruthless enough to do only what is needed to make the final pass and score. Then at the restart, in your mind, wind the score back to 0–0, secure the ball and don't let the opposition strike back straight away.

Clever tactics

Game plans should be based on clever tactics worked out before the match starts, but how clever can tactics be? Once, a match was to be played in freezing conditions. One of the coaches (ex All Black selector, the late Gordon Hunter, who co-authored a previous edition of this book) obtained plastic bin liners, cut holes for the arms and got the players to wear these under their shirts. Warm as toast, they annihilated the shivering opposition.

At the 2003 Rugby World Cup the All Blacks seemed unstoppable but, in the semi-final, the Australians decided the All Blacks had a weakness at centre. They kept bringing their wings in to attack it, and frustrated the All Blacks by starving them of possession. In the end, Australia won an unexpected victory.

Know all of the above and use it exactly as needed during the course of a game. Be resilient in disaster; be vigilant after success . . . the winner is the team that has the most points *at the end of the game*.

Imagine this: After putting in a mountain of hard work, you are ahead by 5 points, in possession, with three minutes left on the clock. Now is time to close out the game. Wind it down with a series of rucks and mauls with the ball taken up by your forwards, always keeping the ball tight and not kicking possession away to the opposition. Then, when time is up, put the ball out of play. At last the referee blows his whistle.

That is when you celebrate your triumph.

17 THE LAWS

The rules of rugby are set by the International Rugby Board (IRB). Twenty-two of them are listed here, laid out in a natural sequence — before the match, during the match, in the field of play, restarts and in-goal. They start with the ground you play on and end with you grounding the ball in the in-goal. Try!

A full set of laws is available and downloadable from **irb.com/laws**. If you want to clarify a ruling, go to the particular law (for example, Law 8 Advantage) and then find the subheading that matches your question.

On the website, you can also watch video clips and digital animations of the laws in practice. Individual countries often have variations of the laws, especially for age-group rugby, so refer to their websites for these. Some country's websites are listed in the useful addresses section on pages 164–165 of this book.

NOTE: As mentioned, the aspects of the main laws are threaded into the text of this book where they occur and are most relevant. What follows is to highlight some unusual situations in the laws only. In any dispute, always refer to the actual law in the original IRB document.

Those who are ignorant of, or who break the laws, end up in the sin bin.

BEFORE THE MATCH

Law 1: The ground
The 22-metre zone
The special rules that apply to the 22-metre zone are a player can kick directly out of it to touch; a player can mark a ball kicked by an opponent; and 22-metre dropouts are taken from behind the 22-metre line.

Law 2: The ball
The ball must be oval, made of four panels, in the dimensions shown (smaller for youth rugby). It may be treated to make it water-resistant and easier to grip.

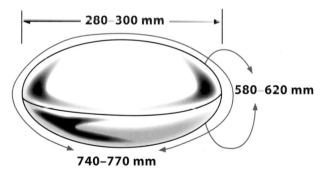

280–300 mm

580–620 mm

740–770 mm

Law 3: Number of players
A maximum of 15 players are allowed on the field for each team, with seven replacements/substitutes. A replacement temporarily replaces an injured teammate. A substitute permanently replaces a teammate for tactical reasons. A player who is substituted can't come back on the field (except to temporarily replace a player in the blood bin).

Injured players, substitutions & blood bins

A referee can order off players for medical attention. If bleeding, they must go to the blood bin and can be temporarily replaced. If off the field for more than 15 minutes of actual time, they cannot return. If the temporary replacement is sin binned, the player in the blood bin can't return until the sin bin is finished.

Front-row forward variations

There must be at least three front-row players on the field to contest the scrums (and two off it if there are seven replacements). So a permanently substituted front-row forward can return to replace a player who is in the blood bin or the sin bin (temporarily), or who has been sent off (permanently), so that scrums can be contested. But in the case of a sin bin or sending off, another teammate must leave the field.

Front-row forwards letting off steam.

Can't return & uncontested

However, a front-row forward who has been sin binned can't return even temporarily until their sin bin is complete, or if sent off, can't return at all. If there are not enough front-row forwards, the referee orders uncontested scrums. In an uncontested scrum the teams do not compete for the ball; the team throwing in the ball must win it, and neither team is allowed to push.

Law 4: Players' clothing

No player can leave the playing area to change items of clothing (unless bloodstained), so if you rip your shorts — you have to change them on the field!

Law 5: Time

A referee can end a match at any time, if they believe it would be dangerous to continue.

Law 6: Match officials

When the ref gets in the way

If the ball or the ball carrier touches the referee in the field of play and one team gets an advantage out of it, the ref orders a scrum and the team that last played the ball has the throw-in. If there is no advantage, it's play on. But, get this — if the attacking team has the ball in the in-goal and the ref gets in the way, he has to award a try. If it's a defending player, he has to award a touch down.

Some other fool gets in the way

Only players, match officials, the match doctor and the non-playing members of the team may enter the playing area. But let's say an idiot or a dog touches the ball in the in-goal area, then the ref has to work out what happens next — either award a try or a touch down at the place where the ball was touched.

DURING THE MATCH

Law 7: Mode of play

Law 8: Advantage

Advantage is played to make play continuous and it must be clear and real; how long it is played is at the discretion of the referee.

Law 9: Methods of scoring

Not from another body, but the wind is fine

With a goal attempt, if, after the ball is kicked, it touches the ground or any teammate of the kicker, a goal cannot be scored. However, if the ball is touched only by the wind, which blows it back after it has crossed the crossbar, a goal is scored.

Law 10: Foul play

Law 11: Offside & onside in general play

Law 12: Knock-on or throw forwards

If a knock-on or throw forwards is unintentional, a scrum is awarded to the opposition. If it is intentional, a penalty is awarded.

IN THE FIELD OF PLAY

Law 13: Kickoff & restart kicks

Law 14: Ball on the ground — no tackle

Law 15: Tackle — Ball Carrier brought to Ground

Law 16: Ruck

Law 17: Maul

Law 18: Mark

Law 19: Touch & line out

Law 20: Scrum

The minimum number of players allowed in a scrum is five.

Law 21: Penalty & free kicks

Penalty or free kick in the in-goal

If a player retires into in-goal to take a penalty or free kick awarded in the field of play and a defending player, by foul play, prevents an opponent from scoring a try, a penalty try is awarded.

IN-GOAL

Law 22: In-goal

GLOSSARY

5-metre scrum — a scrum 5 metres (5½ yards) from the defending team's goal line.

10-metre line — the line either side of the halfway line past which the ball has to be kicked at a kickoff.

22-metre dropout — a drop kick to restart play that is taken by the defending team from behind their 22-metre line (22 metres is around 24 yards).

22-metre line — the line on the field of play that marks a team's defensive zone (also called the 22).

Acting scrum half — player acting as scrum half at a ruck or maul.

Advantage — when the referee allows play to continue because the non-offending team has possession of the ball and they have gained a clear advantage.

Against the head — winning the ball at the scrum when the other team has put it in.

Ankle tap — striking the ball-carrier's ankle from behind, causing a loss of balance.

"Anything goes" pass — any pass, no matter how awkward, that reaches the receiver.

Back line — the line of backs waiting to defend or attack.

Backs — the players who stand behind the scrum (*see also* Forwards & backs, page 24).

Back row — three outside (loose) players in the scrum.

Back three — the fullback and the two wings.

Ball carrier — the person carrying the ball.

Binding — Grasping firmly another player's body between the shoulders and the hips with the whole arm in contact from hand to shoulder.

Blind side — the space between the ball and the nearest touchline (compare open side).

Blind-side charge — an attacking move on the blind side of the field.

Blind-side defence — defence on the blind side of the field.

Bobbing ball — the ball bouncing along the ground unevenly.

Body position — the alignment of the whole body when carrying out a technique.

Box kick — a high kick aimed so the ball lands in front of the opposing wing.

Breakdown — when possession of the ball has been temporarily halted and is being contested by both sides. A tackle is usually the point of breakdown.

Bump [off] — the ball carrier knocks back the tackler by bumping a shoulder against their shoulder.

Cavalry charge — a type of illegal charge by group of players.

Centre — playing position in the middle of the back line.

Change-of-direction pass — pretending to pass in one direction, then passing in the opposite direction instead.

Channel — a route between the players' legs taken by the ball when it is coming back through the scrum (there are three main channels).

Chip kick or **Chip-and-chase kick** — a short kick over an opponent's head.

Code — secret signals or messages a team uses to communicate planned moves.

Conversion — the kick at goal following a try.

Corner flag — the flags at the corners of the goal line and the touchline.

Counter-attack — an attacking move in response to an opposition attack after possession has changed hands.

Cross kick — a kick across the field towards the attacking team's open wing position.

Cut-back pass — a pass to a player who cuts back in the opposite direction (also called a scissors pass).

Cut-out pass — a pass that misses out a player in the attacking team and is intended for the next player out (also called a miss-out pass).

Dart — a sudden movement in a different direction.

Dead — The ball is out of play.

Dead-ball line — the line at each end of the field of play. When the ball or the player carrying the ball touches it, the ball is said to be "dead".

Decoy — a player who pretends to be about to get the ball to confuse the opposition.

Defence — the system, tactics or actions used to counter an opposition attack.

Delaying the pass — the ball carrier holding on to the ball longer than usual before passing to try to break up the rhythm of the defence.

Dive pass — passing the ball while diving towards the catcher.

Dodge — move quickly to the side to avoid a tackler.

Drawing the player — committing an opponent to making the tackle before passing.

Drift defence — a system of defence that drifts sideways across the field.

Drive — to push forwards by driving the legs hard against the ground.

Driving maul — a maul in which the opposition is driven back.

Driving tackle — when the tackler pushes the ball carrier backwards.

Drop goal — a drop kick from the field of play that sends the ball over the crossbar.

Drop kick — the ball dropped from the hand or hands to the ground and kicked as it rises from its first bounce.

Dropout — a restart of play in which the defending team drop-kicks from behind their own 22-metre line.

Drubber — a short, flat kick (also called a grubber kick).

Dummy or Dummy pass — a pretend pass.

Dummy kick — a pretend kick.

Engagement — when the opposing front rows of the scrum come together.

Extra time — time added on by the referee for injuries and stoppages.

Fair catch — a player catching the ball inside their own 22 when the opposition has kicked it (also called a mark).

Fast pass — when the ball is passed as soon as it is caught because the receiver is about to be tackled.

Feint — a fake move to deceive an opponent.

Fend — when the ball carrier uses the arm and open hand to push off an opponent (also called a hand-off).

Field of play — the whole of the playing field between the two dead-ball lines.

First five-eighth — the fly half.

Flanker — one of the two players on either side, or flank, in the third, or back, row of the scrum (also called a wing forward).

Flick pass — a pass using a flick of the wrist.

Fly half — the back who stands between the scrum half and the inside centre.

Forward charge — an aggressive run by a forward with the ball in which the player tries to knock opponents out of the way.

Forward pass   when a player throws a pass towards the front. This is an illegal move in rugby.

Foul play — play that is dangerous or against the rules or the spirit of the game.

Free kick — a lesser-grade penalty which allows a team a free kick of the ball. See penalty.

Front-on tackle — a tackle in which the ball carrier runs straight at the tackler.

Front row — the first row of forwards in the scrum, consisting of two props and a hooker.

Fullback — the player nearest to the team's own goalposts.

Full stop — to suddenly stop dead with the ball, usually done to confuse the opposition.

Full time — the end of the match.

Gain line — an imaginary line between the two teams that must be crossed for one team to gain a territorial advantage over the other.

Gang tackle — two or more opposing players tackling the ball carrier.

Garryowen — the up-and-under kick, named after an Irish club that used it frequently.

General play — not set play.

Goal — a successful kick between the goalposts.

Goal line — the line the goals are on (also called the try line).

Goalposts — the upright posts that make up the goal.

Goose step — a short step with the knees locked.

Grounding — forcing the ball against the ground in the in-goal area with the hands, arms or upper body.

Grubber — a short, flat kick (also called a drubber kick).

Gum shield — a plastic guard that is placed in the mouth over the upper row of teeth (also called a mouth guard).

Hack kick — a kick ahead of the loose ball.

Halfback — the back who stands closest to the scrum (also called the scrum half).

Halfback pass — a long pass from the forwards to the backs.

Half hold — when the ball carrier is held but not fully tackled.

Hand-off — when the ball carrier uses the arm and open hand to push off an opponent (also called a fend).

High tackle — a dangerous and illegal tackle above the line of the shoulders.

Hindmost foot — the last foot of the last player in a scrum, ruck, maul etc.

Hit and spin — a forward charge in which the ball carrier manages to spin out of the tackle.

Hooker — the player who hooks back the ball in the scrum.

Hospital pass — a poorly timed pass that reaches the catcher at the same time as the tackler (thus risking injury).

In-goal — the area of the field between the goalposts and the dead-ball line.

Infringement — any action that breaks the laws.

Inside centre — centre closest to the scrum.

In touch — off the field of play.

Jump — to leap vertically off the ground, usually to catch the ball.

Kickoff — the start of a match or the restart after one team has scored.

Knock-on — when the ball has struck a player's hands or arms, gone forwards, then hit the ground or another player.

Line out — the players lined up to catch the ball when it is thrown back onto the field.

Line-out calls — the coded calls telling the jumpers of the team throwing in where the ball is going.

Lob pass — a pass over an opponent's head.

Lock — one of the two second-row forwards in the middle of the scrum.

Long pass — a longer than normal pass across the field.

Loop — when a player runs around a teammate they have just passed to in order to receive the ball back again.

Loosehead prop — the prop on the left side of the team's own scrum.

Loosie — a common name for the three players of the back row of the scrum who are able to disengage more quickly than the tight five. They are the players expected to be first to the loose ball or breakdown.

Mark — 1. The place from which a penalty, free kick or scrum is taken. 2. A defender catching the ball from an opposition kick inside their own 22 (also called a fair catch).

Marking — watching and staying with an opponent, ready to tackle.

Maul — a wrestle for the ball between both teams.

Miss-out pass — a pass that misses out one attacking player and is meant for the next player in the line (also called a cut-out pass).

Mobile — being able to move rapidly around the field.

Mouth guard — a plastic guard that is placed in the mouth over the upper row of teeth (also called a gum shield).

Non-offending team — the team that has not broken a law (compare offending).

Non-pass — when the ball carrier changes speed or direction as if about to pass but doesn't pass and speeds up again.

Normal pass — the normal pass made by a running player using a swing of the arms and body to pass the ball to a teammate.

Number eight/no. 8 — the player at the back of the scrum.

Obstruction — illegally getting in the way of an opposition player.

Offending team — the team that has broken a law (compare non-offending).

Offside — when a player is standing where prohibited, usually in front of the ball.

One-handed pass — passing the ball with one hand.

One-handed tap back — a line-out jumper knocking the ball back towards the team's own side with one hand.

Onside — being in a fair position, usually behind the ball.

Open play — when play is moving around the field without being stopped by the referee.

Open rugby — fast, flowing rugby.

Open side — the space between the ball and the farthest touchline (compare blind side).

Out — off the field of play.

Outside centre — the centre who stands farthest from the team's own scrum.

Outside cut — a swerve towards the outside of the field.

Outside-in defence — when the defenders nearest the touchline mark opposition players standing in from them.

Overhead pass — when a player lifts the ball above the head to get the pass over the head of a tackler.

Over-the-shoulder kick — a kick, often made by the scrum half, when facing the wrong way and under pressure from the opposition.

Over-the-top throw — a long throw that goes right over the top of the line out.

Overlap — when one side has an extra player on the outside.

Pass — when a player throws the ball to a teammate.

Passing on — when the ball is quickly passed out towards the wings.

Peel — a move in which a forward runs the ball up from the line out.

Penalty — a higher-grade penalty which allows a team a free kick of the ball and the rights to take a penalty kick at goal or kick the ball directly into touch and receive the throw at the line out. See free kick.

Penalty try — a try awarded by the referee when the attacking team would have scored but for foul play by the opposition.

Penetrator — an attacking player who breaks through the defence of the opposition.

Phase play — play punctuated by rucks and mauls.

Pick-and-go — a forward charge in which the ball is put on the ground in the tackle and the next forward picks it up and runs with it.

Pivot — a player who sets up a penetration move. Also another name for the fly half.

Place kick — kicking the ball after it is placed on the ground.

Player-on-player defence — a system of defence in which the tackler takes the player directly opposite.

Player-out defence — a system of defence in which the tacklers line up their players from the outside of the field inward.

Pop pass — a very short pass.

Positions — where the players stand on the field, which is fixed in set play.

Prop — the players in the scrum who support the hooker.

Punt — to kick the ball from the hand.

Push-over try — a try scored as a result of the attacking team pushing their opponent's scrum over their own goal line.

Quality ball — good, clean possession that can be used to create an attack.

Quick throw-in — a throw into the line out taken quickly before the line out has formed.

Referee — the official on the field who ensures both teams keep to the laws of the game.

Replacement — player who temporarily replaces an injured teammate.

Retire — to resume an onside position, either behind a teammate about to kick the ball or 10 metres (11 yards) from an opposing player about to take a free kick or penalty.

Reverse flick — a pass thrown backwards by the ball carrier to a teammate in behind.

Ripping the ball — pulling the ball free at a maul (also called stripping the ball).

Rolling maul — a maul in which the attacking team constantly changes the point of attack to the left or the right while going forwards.

Ruck — when the ball is on the ground and both teams are trying to push each other off it.

Rules — the agreed laws on how the game will be played.

Scissors pass — passing to a player who cuts back in the opposite direction (also known as a cut-back pass).

Screw kick — a kick that causes the ball to spin through the air (also called a spiral kick).

Scrum or Scrummage — a set-piece pushing contest between two teams.

Scrum half — the player closest to the scrum (also called the halfback).

Scrum-half pass — a long pass by the scrum half to clear the ball from the forwards to the backs.

Scrum machine — a machine used at scrum practice for the forwards to practise pushing against. It can be made with weights attached to a homemade sled.

Second five-eighth — the inside centre.

Second phase — when both teams are contesting possession of the ball.

Second row — the two locks, who form the second row of forwards in the scrum.

Set piece or Set play — a set way of restarting play, such as a scrum or line out.

Shortened line out — when the team throwing in calls for fewer than seven players to take part in the line out.

Side-on tackle — a tackle made into the side of the ball carrier.

Side step — to evade a tackler by quickly stepping to one side before proceeding.

Sin bin — when a player must leave the field for 10 minutes for illegal play.

Smother tackle — a type of tackle in which the ball-carrier's arms are held, or smothered, so the ball can't be passed.

Spin — the rotation of the ball as it is propelled through the air.

Spin pass — a pass that causes the ball to spin through the air (also called a spiral pass).

Spiral kick — a kick that causes the ball to spiral through the air (also called a screw kick).

Spiral pass — a pass that causes the ball to spiral through the air (also called a spin pass).

Stationary tackle — a tackle made when the ball carrier is running at a tackler who is standing still.

Stiff-arm tackle — a dangerous tackle made with the arms straight.

Stripping the ball — pulling the ball free at a maul (also called ripping the ball).

Swerve — to deviate from a straight line, usually at speed.

Substitute — player who permanently replaces a teammate for tactical reasons.

Super Rugby — the regional tournament played between teams in the southern hemisphere.

Support — to follow closely; to back up the ball carrier.

Tackle — to stop the ball carrier and (usually) take them to the ground.

Tackled-ball pass — a pass made by a ball carrier who has been tackled but still has one or both hands free.

Tactics — a way of working as a team to beat the opposition.

Tap kick or Tap penalty — a short penalty kick used when the attacking team intends to run with the ball.

Technique — the exact means of achieving one's purpose.

Three-quarter — the centres and wings.

Throw forwards — when the ball is thrown, deliberately or accidentally, in the direction of the opposition goal line (not level or backwards). It is illegal and results in a penalty.

Tight five — the name given to the tightly bound front and second-row forwards who do the hard, or tight, work in the scrums, line outs, rucks and mauls.

Tight forward — a forward in the front or second row who does most of the "heavy" work, such as at scrums, rucks and mauls.

Tighthead — hooking the ball in the scrum when the other team has put it in.

Tighthead prop — the prop on the right side of the team's own scrum, farthest away from where the scrum half puts the ball in.

Touch or Touchline — the lines at the side of the field of play. When they are touched by the ball or the player carrying it, the ball is said to be out.

Touch down — a defender grounding the ball in the team's own in-goal area.

Touch judge — the official on the touchline who signals when the ball is out.

Touchline tackle — a tackle that pushes or drives the ball carrier over the touchline.

Truck and trailer — a rolling maul where the team with the ball has separated into two groups: the forward group (without the ball) illegally protecting the second group, which has the ball.

Try — the grounding of the ball by an attacking player in the opponent's in-goal area.

Try line — the line on or beyond which a try is scored (also called the goal line).

Unit — a small group of players working together.

Upright — one of the posts that make up the goalposts.

Up-and-under — a high kick to test or put pressure on the opposition (also called a Garryowen).

Wheel — when a scrum moves through more than 90 degrees.

Willie-away — a peel from the line out, named after New Zealander Wilson Whineray (see also peel).

Wing or Wing three-quarter — the players closest to the touchlines.

Wing forward — another name for a flanker.

Wipers kick — an angled kick across the field (with an angle similar to that of a windshield wiper).

INDEX